Pocket Pearls
Biblically-Based Practical Wisdom for the Heart

by
Reverend Willette O. Wright

Dearest Dottye:

Grace and peace to be
you. It is difficult to
put in words how very much I
have and appreciate you. Your friendship
has been a blessing to me and has inspired me
me as a preacher. From the day I first met you,
I was encouraged and inspired as a woman and
pastor, as a preacher. You are the epitome of grace
and wisdom for so many. I pray that Porket & Pearls
will be a blessing to you. I also pray that as you read
you will see reflection of how your example has been
a blessing to me. I also pray that God's presence
blessings for you and your family!

Love,
William

Dedication

This book is dedicated to the memory of my husband, Reverend Steven Kenneth Wright. Thank you for the Pearls. I am doing all that I can to live by them and with them until we meet again in Heaven. I love you.

This book is also lovingly dedicated to my Mommee, Constance Wright. I have often referred to you as my Naomi. Thank you for surrendering your life to the Lord Jesus Christ as a young mother. That started the process of bringing up your children and especially my beloved Steve in the nurture and admonition of the Lord. Thank you for having been the example of Christ to Steve in his early years and for putting him in a church where he could receive the baptism with the Holy Spirit. Thank you for being a wife who allowed her husband to be the example of a man and bring his son up to be a faithful man. Thank you for staying with me and not leaving me when Steve went home. I am forever grateful and indebted to you for being such a godly woman and constant friend.

I am blessed beyond measure to have been born into what I think is the best family in the world — the Oliver family. This book is dedicated to the memory of my parents, William and Mollie Oliver, and to my siblings. Thank you Mamma and Daddy for being the best parents anyone could have. Thank you for staying together and raising your children to do the same. Thank you for instilling in me a love for learning and serving. Thank you for taking me to church so that I could learn about Jesus and give my life to Him.

To my brothers and sisters, thank you for making 327 56th Street and 1011 Nova Avenue a haven for becoming a tribe to be reckoned with. We are, and always will be, Daddy's "Magnificent Seven." To the road crew (you know who you are), I think trips to South Carolina put the "road trip" bug in us! May we always ride together!

A Note of Thanks

I am immensely grateful and blessed beyond measure to have been shepherded by two pastors who, along with their wives, have lovingly helped me grow spiritually. First, I am grateful for Episcopal Pastor John A. Cherry and Reverend Diana P. Cherry of From the Heart Church Ministries Worldwide ™. Thank you for nurturing me when I was a babe in Christ, guiding Steve and me through pre-marital counseling, marrying us at the "right time," and showing us how to be ministers. Thank you for "being there" when I needed you most. Secondly, thank you Bishop John A. Cherry, II and Reverend LaWanda Cherry for continuing to build upon the spiritual foundation that was laid by our Episcopal Pastor. I am blessed to be a part of your lives. From standing with you when you "became one," to ministering with you as you lead the From the Heart family, it is an honor to serve with you. You continue to provide an example of love and marriage that this world so desperately needs. I love and appreciate you.

For 34 years, I have been blessed to be a member of a good church. In those years, there have been many people who have deposited into my life and allowed me to grow as a preacher. Thank you to my From the Heart Church family. Steve and I would not have been able to do what God called us to do without your love and support. You are the best!

Friendships come and go, but real friendships stand the test of time. A very special thank you to my friend, Toni Foxx. Thank you for being my "big sister" and for loving me and my family through it all. You have mourned with us, cried with us, laughed with us, and celebrated with us. I am especially grateful for your "mother wit" and your constant encouragement to finish this book. Thank you also for being the best copy editor — I could not have done it without you!

Table of Contents

Part Three: Pocket Pearls
and the "Nevers"

Introduction

This book is written in an effort to capture the significance and the beauty of a life lived after having found the Pearl of Great Price — salvation through Jesus Christ. It is about the life of a man named Steven Kenneth Wright, a strong yet personable man whose great intellect and deep spirituality were encased in a kind and loving heart full of wit and humor. After receiving Jesus Christ as his Lord and Saviour, God gave Steve twelve spiritual Pearls to live with and to live by for a successful and richly fulfilled life. He did just that and then, at the age of 36, he died. He was a son, a brother, a husband and a preacher. For me, his wife, he was a man too young to die and too great an example to be missing from our lives.

At a very young age, my husband found the Pearl of Great Price. He received Jesus Christ as his personal Lord and Saviour at the age of 11. Throughout his life, God deposited in him simple truths from the scriptures which he chose to call "Pearls." My husband lived by the Pearls and they caused him to be an example, a role model, a standard, and a pattern to the many people he served. He was a man of impeccable character and a preacher of God's Word.

Reverend Wright was a native of Washington, DC. Throughout his schooling, he was an excellent student and upon graduation from high school, he attended American University. There, his excellent Christian character led him to become a Bible study teacher and leader, a musician with the Gospel Choir, and a friend and colleague to many local pastors and preachers. He even played football for the University. I am told that as a football player he had skill. Because of his quick and nimble moves on the field he was given the name "Cha Cha."

Even before his years at American University, Steve was a teacher of God's Word. He grew up in a church where his family was actively involved and his uncle was the pastor. By the time I met my husband at the age of 24, he had been preaching the Word of God and leading souls to Jesus Christ in his high school, his church, on his college campus, on the streets of Washington, DC, and anywhere opportunity was given. My husband loved God and the Word of God.

In the very early years of his ministry with our church, my husband sensed God calling him to three days of prayer and fasting to gain insight and direction. In those three days, the Pearls were defined and written on paper as they had been so clearly written in Steve's heart. God told him to live these Pearls and to use them to guide his life and ministry. Although I did not understand them then, for ten years as his wife I saw the Pearls come alive. Because he lived them and because I have had to live [with] them without him, I now understand and appreciate them. I know that my life is richer, fuller, and more productive because of them.

Over the years, I have grown to understand why the Pearls given to my husband were so valuable to him and such a necessary part of his life. I have realized within the 20 years since his passing that his life was and is such a necessary influence on me as a wife and such a loving force in the lives of the people he knew and loved. I believe that the Pearls given to him by God were an essential part of his development as a Christian and as a man. That is what I hope to share with you in this book. The Pearls are simple truths from the Word of God that have an extraordinary effect on living a life that is well pleasing to God and becoming a source of love for others.

You may ask why this book is called Pocket Pearls. Typically, pearls are worn to adorn the outer body so that their beauty may be seen by those who admire them. Unlike natural pearls, the twelve spiritual Pearls given to my husband can only be displayed once they have been buried deep within the heart. A shirt pocket is typically placed over the heart of the one wearing it. Its content, though unseen with the natural eye, is at all times close to the heart. These Pearls are to be received and worn from the heart. According to Proverbs 4:23, one must, *"Keep and guard your heart with all vigilance and above all that you guard, for out of it flow the springs of life"* (Amplified Version). This scripture tells us that what goes into the heart must be carefully determined because the heart is the starting point for the activities of life. Pocket Pearls are Biblically-based practical wisdom for the heart.

Whatever you may be wearing as you read this book, it is my prayer that, with each page, you will decide to place these invaluable Pearls in the pocket that is your heart. It does not matter whether you are male or female, these Pearls are not related to gender, race, color or creed. They are not presented to be associated with any fashion trend or statement, religious commitment, political affiliation, or psychological mental model. They are truly jewels for your soul and ornaments for your mind. Should you receive them and wear them daily, they will make you wise and cause you to live a life well pleasing to God. That's what they did in my husband's life and it is what they continue to do in mine.

Chapter One

The Life of Reverend Steven Kenneth Wright

Again, the kingdom of heaven is like unto a merchant man, seeking goodly pearls: who, when he had found one pearl of great price, went and sold all that he had, and bought it (Matthew 13:45-46).

I have never had a great appreciation for pearls; however, I think they are beautiful. There is something about the way they become what they are. They are born out of frustration and irritation. A tiny almost unnoticeable living organism struggles against a wall of difficulty and resistance until finally, a hard yet rich substance is made.

Even the process by which the pearl is discovered is painstaking. Pressure must be applied in order to free the beautiful creation from its stifling bed of development. The phenomenon that is the beginning of one of the most beautiful and precious substances is often untold. Once found, a pearl may be of great value or of little value. Ultimately, it is up to the person who desires its beauty to seek diligently for a pearl of great worth or value.

My lack of appreciation for pearls was evident when I was preparing for my wedding day. As I hastily considered how I would be adorned as a bride, I did not want to wear pearls (as they seemed to be old-fashioned) but I thought wearing them was the "proper" thing to do. I remember thinking that pearls represented purity and femininity. I also remember thinking that if I wore them, they had to be "real" or "genuine." With a very limited wedding budget, I soon realized that the cost of real or genuine pearls was beyond my reach.

In my naivety about pearls and my determination to wear the real thing, I learned that fresh water pearls, although genuine, were less expensive and, to some extent, equally as beautiful. I also learned that most pearls were cultivated; that is, some intervention by man was necessary to create the beautiful gem. Given my budget and the abundant availability of different types of pearls,

I purchased a necklace and earrings made from fresh water pearls. They were small and not very noticeable; but to me, they were real jewels for the most significant day of my life. On my wedding day, I wore the dainty fresh water pearls that I hoped were beautiful enough to make my husband smile, the wedding pictures classic, and my friends and family members happy. Those natural pearls were a small yet necessary part of the story of my life with a man who would one day leave me with spiritual Pearls that would help me to live a fulfilled and Christ-like life.

I met my husband at church. He once told me that he had checked me out during church and had intentions of introducing himself and asking me out. However, he saw me arrive with several friends during one of our many group fellowships and thought that one of them was "the man in my life." Once he completed a thorough investigation and found out that I was not at all "attached," he decided to pursue me.

While we met in church, shortly after meeting I took a professorship at a university in North Carolina. I did not know at the time that my husband's intentions for me were beyond friendship. We started communicating through letters and when I received the first letter from him, I was smitten. It was not a romantic letter but it was so very warm and friendly. Even more engaging for me was the fact that the letter was well written with excellent penmanship. To me, it and every letter thereafter was a work of art; a masterpiece that eloquently and clearly allowed him to be with me even while we were more than 200 miles apart. I was impressed and his letter writing and beautiful penmanship caught my attention and captured my heart. There was something about the way he expressed himself. Even without seeing his face or audibly hearing him speak, in my mind I could envision his every expression and hear his calming voice as I carefully read each page over and over again. Although our courtship was "across the miles," our relationship grew quickly and deeply. While we grew to like and love each other and commit to becoming man and wife, I know that our relationship was as strong as it was because we were first committed to a personal relationship with the Lord through Jesus Christ.

We were married after a two-year courtship which included a series of intense pre-marital counseling sessions. With little money and new jobs for both of us, we began our lives together with great anticipation for what was to come. We were both employed with jobs in our respective fields of study; he was a scientist and I was a speech pathologist. We had a little house that was just enough for us and we were "in love." We had settled into what we hoped would be a long and beautiful life together as husband and wife.

After a little less than one year of marriage, my husband accepted a position in full-time ministry with our church. I believe that, in his heart, he always knew that serving the Lord through full-time ministry was his destiny. Although he loved microbiology and the scientific process, his passion for the Word of God and his genuine concern for the lives of the people we served grew greater with every year of marriage. Shortly after my husband started working for the church, I joined him. At first, I struggled with the idea of forsaking my lofty goal of working in Higher Education. I had set my sights on becoming the president of some college or university. After very little prompting and one of our many family meetings, it was my husband's gentle, yet persuasive, admonishment to surrender to "working for the church" that swayed me. I soon grew to love working with my husband. He taught science in the ministry's Christian School and I worked in the Christian Education Department. Once again, we settled into our professional roles and looked forward to working together.

For just about nine years, we shared office space, had lunch together, worked late hours together, married couples, dedicated babies, counseled, developed and administered programs, prayed, and served together. With all of the togetherness, as is the case I believe with all marriages, each of the nine years of working together was not without the challenges and obstacles couples face. As dedicated and as committed as we were to what God called us to do, we were human beings. There were times when we disagreed, didn't speak and even raised our voices (mine more than his), but we did it together. Even with the challenges, to me, it was perfect.

Our perfect life was shaken when after about eight years of marriage, it was discovered that my husband had an irregular heartbeat. Before the diagnosis, he was usually involved in sports and other physical activity; we did not have any indication that something was wrong. He found out about the irregular heartbeat after one of our church members, who is a physician, casually yet consistently suggested to him that he needed to get a physical. Like many men, my husband was not fond of doctor visits. Because he exercised and usually felt fine, he leaned more towards taking vitamins, getting rest and every now and then, indulging me by participating in a cleansing or fitness fast. After second or third suggestions from Dr. Wilson, my husband went in for a physical, which led to a series of tests that ultimately resulted in a couple of hospitalizations.

Even while going through the tests and evaluations to determine the status of his heart, Steve continued to work and do most of the things he was accustomed to doing. That physical was the beginning of a two-year period that included one incident where my husband collapsed during a meeting in a city about an hour away from home. That day, I received a phone call from one of the participants in the meeting who had called 911. I was shaking and afraid of what might have happened. I rushed to the hospital where he had been taken only to find him sitting in bed smiling. I was at wit's end. I was always more worried about his health and well being than it appeared he was. My husband was very nonchalant about the tests, evaluations, and medications. He consistently told me that it was "okay" and that if he died he would see Jesus. I really wanted to have that kind of faith and confidence with no fear of death. At the time, I did not. I was afraid but I did what was necessary to smile and have the devoted wife presence while trying to agree with what he said. We were young and I did not want to think about the possibility of death. Life was great, we were settled and it was perfect; no room for anything other than the perfect life.

On December 7, 1994, my fears were realized. That morning, my husband and I had a bit of a disagreement concerning something that I cannot remember now. What I do remember is that by the time we were dressed to go to work, we were good. We had agreed to disagree. He would be leaving that day to go on an annual Men's Retreat. After I had been at work for a short time, my husband came to my office to make sure that we were okay. We laughed about our conversation from the morning and we kissed, hugged (a real good one) and said, "I love you." As was usually the case, I tried to mother him by reminding him of taking his medicine, not letting his feet get wet if there was snow, and my final insistence — "don't play basketball; you shouldn't exert yourself too much." He laughed, kissed me again and said "okay." I knew he didn't mean it so I found the minister with whom he would be traveling that day. I asked him to do what I knew my husband would not do. I simply said, "take care of my husband." Reverend Branson knew about my husband's health challenge and assured me that he would do what was necessary to keep him in check.

After I had settled into the work of the day, I was in a meeting with the pastor when my husband knocked on the door and asked to see me once again. He said he just wanted to see me again before they pulled off. I was especially happy about one more opportunity to say, "I love you, be careful and call me as soon as you get there." His last goodbye also gave opportunity for one more of those wonderful hugs and for him to pinch my cheeks. I don't know why but he loved to pinch my cheeks. He said they were made for pinching and they are "so cute." I always fussed about him doing it but I always allowed it. My fussing was just a ploy that allowed me to bask in the wonder of my husband's love for me. I thank God for that moment. It is etched in my mind because it is how I remember my husband — tall, smiling, caring, and loving.

Several hours after that hug and kiss, I received a phone call saying that something had happened on the way to the retreat. The first call was from one of our co-workers, Brother Paul Henderson. The second call was from the minister whom I had asked to take care of my husband. He simply said, "I think you need to get here." I was panic stricken and yet, I thought this time would be like the time before when he had collapsed. I was prepared to travel for quite some time only to find my husband in a hospital smiling and trying to allay my concern. It did not happen that way. I left the church praying and hoping that my husband was okay. I was accompanied by my brother-in-law Kirk as we drove in the direction of the retreat facility. We were not really sure what hospital he had been taken but were hopeful to get more information from the church along the way. We were driving without a specific destination because we wanted to get there. After almost an hour of driving, I called the church to ask if anyone had gotten word about what had happened and where Steve had been taken. When she answered the phone, my pastor's secretary did not answer my question. The next voice I heard was that of my pastor saying, "come back to me Willette." Those words struck my heart like a sharp knife; my chest hurt and I felt like I couldn't breathe. I knew without knowing that my husband was gone. I did not want to think it and I would not believe it. But I had to turn around and go back home without reaching my husband.

My husband died that day and I was not with him. Of course, in my mind, my husband's death came too soon. I thought about how perfect things were, about how optimistic we had become after the last hospitalization. We had prayed, we had fasted, we had believed God. The Friday before his death, we had even received good news from his new Cardiologist. She said that his heart had miraculously gotten better. This day was too much; it was quick, a sudden absence that just did not make sense. We had just been sitting in the bathroom agreeing to disagree. How could he be gone?

We had experienced many of the obstacles and challenges that are a part of being married and had weathered them. As a young couple, we did not expect that we would have to deal with the "in sickness" part of the wedding vows. I thought that part of the vows would not have to be dealt with until we were old and gray. I thought that we were working to build a marriage, a family, and a ministry that would afford us an opportunity to be an example to the world. In my eyes, God had given me the best husband on the planet; he was mine and we were going to do great things. We were going to spend the rest of our lives preaching the Word of God and in the golden years of retirement, according to my husband, we were going to vacation on "the beaches of the world." This could not be happening.

I was not prepared to lose my best friend and revered confidant. Nothing can describe or explain the sudden and horrible sense of emptiness and despair that shrouds the heart and mind when you lose the love of your life. In the days following his death, I struggled to find a way to feel his presence, to have some tangible sense of nearness to him. I could not believe and did not want to grasp with my mind the horrible thought of living without him.

In spite of what I felt, the reality was that my husband went to Heaven and I had to live without him. Living without his physical presence required that I keep the memories because they were all I had. However, the memories often gave rise to a question that fueled feelings and thoughts of abandonment. When those memories flooded my mind, I wondered how I would continue to build the life we were supposed to build together.

After almost 20 years, I have chosen to write about the answer to that question. The Pearls are the answer that my husband left for me. He did not leave me with great wealth. He did not leave me with children graced with his infectious smile and full laughter. But he did leave me the Pearls. Steve said, "they are jewels that can make one wise and they are daily keys to renewing the mind and following in the example of Christ's character." He left me everything I needed to continue to live, love, and be fulfilled. By leaving me the Pearls, he left me life lessons and practical Biblical approaches for living my life and building my relationship with the Lord and others. He left me with instructions to go on because he is with Jesus.

I am sharing these Pearls because for too long I treated them as I did natural pearls. I did not fully understand or appreciate the process by which they were acquired and did not regard them as I should have; although I thought they were beautifully demonstrated through my husband's life. His boyish smile and bear hugs encouraged and gave me confidence as a wife. His care and many hours of counsel and wisdom shared with our families were instrumental in leading some of them to salvation and others to greater relationships with the Lord. I will never forget the way he demonstrated unconditional love to the men who were a part of a residential program designed to help them overcome addictions and life challenges. My husband would spend evenings and early morning hours before dawn going into the streets to provide them with shelter and food. There were times when he would empty out our freezer to provide food for the men in the program. The Pearls were the daily keys, tools and reminders for living a Christ-centered life that God used to help him become the man we loved and respected.

His ability to live the Pearls was most evident to me in the way he cared for me as his wife and as a preacher. When I started preaching, my husband taught me how to study to prepare a message, how to put the message together, and how to present the message. He gave himself to me in this regard. He allowed the Word of God as the foundation for each Pearl to cause him to love unconditionally and to give himself in preaching the Word and ministering to any and every one for which an opportunity was given. Now, I have a greater appreciation for these spiritual Pearls because since his death, my experiences have shown that life is full of irritations, frustrations, and difficulties that can only be dealt with through consistent application of the Word of God in a simple and practical manner. That is what the Pearls are for.

The scripture reference quoted earlier in Matthew 13 is a parable or natural story that teaches a spiritual lesson. In this parable, the Pearl of Great Price represents the Kingdom of Heaven. When the merchant man found the Pearl of Great Price, he sold all he had and bought it. For the life of the Christian, not only must the Pearl of Great Price be found, but once it is found, it must be purchased with all that one has. There must be a sacrificial giving of oneself into a relationship with God and in return, what is found is a life characterized by a beauty that only the grace of God can give. After finding the Pearl of Great Price, God graced my husband's life with an amazing and deep love and appreciation for the Scriptures, wisdom beyond his years, and a heart full of Christ-like character. The Pearls are the reflection of this life, the life of Steven Kenneth Wright.

PART ONE

Pocket Pearls As Keys

The Pearls as Keys

The first key I owned was the key to my diary. As a teenage girl I relished the fact that I had my own diary and the key was a sacred part of my life. It unlocked the door to my most private and intimate thoughts. Inside of my dairy were secrets, lies and even hopes and dreams. It was full of images that only a teenager could know and understand. The key to my diary was important to me because it represented access to the "me" that I only expressed in those pages. Access to who I thought I was could only be found by using the little gold key.

I don't remember what happened to that little key or my very important diary. As I grew older I learned that the key was no more than a symbol of safety for my secrets. Anything, a hair pin, a tooth pick, or one of my sister's barrettes, could easily have opened up my treasured secrets for anyone to see.

As a physical key provides the ability to access something, five of the twelve Pearls were given to my husband as keys for unlocking treasures in the heart and providing access to the heart of God. However, unlike a physical key, these keys can never be lost, stolen, or replaced. They provide a way of escape from the material and mundane aspects of life in an ever changing and increasingly evil world.

The following Pearls are keys that must be used daily and consistently. They open our lives and the lives of others to the riches of the Kingdom of God. With these Pearls, one will find and appreciate **loving**, **giving**, **smiles**, and **joy**.

Chapter Two

Pearl One:
The Key to Living is Loving!

In this was manifested the love of God toward us, because that God sent his only begotten Son into the world, that we might live through him (I John 4:9).

To live is more than breathing and having the faculties of one's mind and the use of one's limbs. To live is to know and experience every aspect of freedom that comes with being a living organism created by God and destined to return to God. In this life or living there must be certainty of one's origin through a Creator and one's return to the Creator. You have a natural life because God (the Creator of the universe) has placed a living spirit in a natural body. The spirit on the inside of you is the "real you" — the one who lives a natural life each day. This spirit or real you came from God and will live forever. Our natural lives end when the physical body dies but the real man, the spirit man, lives eternally. Because the spirit of man lives forever and because every human being born has a spirit that will live forever, it is imperative that while we are in a body that is confined to space and time, we use the key to living, which is loving.

The key to living is loving means that in order to really live, one must accept and use the key that unlocks real life. That key is love. God is love and He sent His Son Jesus to be love for us and to demonstrate love to us that we might desire a relationship with Him and have fellowship with Him. The Bible is replete with scriptures that show us this truth. First John 4:9 says, "In *this was manifested the love of God toward us, because that God sent his only begotten Son into the world, that we might live through him."* This truth is also shown in Romans 5:8 which says, *"But God commendeth his love toward us, in that, while we were yet sinners, Christ died for us."*

The focus of this Pearl is to realize that real living takes real loving. First John 4:10-11 says, *"Herein is love, not that we loved God, but that he loved us, and sent his Son to be the propitiation for our sins. Beloved, if God so loved us, we ought also to love one another."* God, the Creator of the universe, loved us so much that He sent His Son to take the punishment for our sins. He sent Jesus to save us from the spiritual death that sin causes. He sent Jesus to deal with and overcome the death that sin brings so that we could live without its burden and guilt. Through and because of God's love for us, real life — freedom from the bondage and shame of sin — is available to everyone who desires it. Love was and is the key to real life.

One of the constants in the world we live in is the desire to find love through meaningful and lasting relationships. There are countless approaches for doing so. Among them is the virtual world of love, which is ever evolving and increasing in use and popularity. The promoters of the world of virtual love suggest that by providing a computer with a little information, a great picture and a few monthly payments, "you too can find love." Marketing and advertising for this approach has worked well. Pew Research suggests that one in ten Americans have used an online dating site or mobile dating app to find a spouse or long-term partner.[1] Research also suggests that general public attitudes towards online dating have become much more positive in recent years. Social networking sites are now playing a prominent role when it comes to navigating and documenting romantic relationships. For many, this approach is a quick and easy way to meet someone and potentially find love.

While the use of virtual methods to finding loving relationships is popular and easily done, research also suggests that negative experiences are relatively common. Pew Research indicates that 54% of online daters felt that persons misrepresented themselves in their personal profiles.[2] Of a more serious concern is that 28% of online daters said that they felt harassed or were uncomfortable with contacts made by someone on an online dating site or app.[3]

The research says that 42% of female online daters have experienced this type of contact at one point or another, compared with 17% of men.[4]

Finding real love and loving requires a greater and more significant approach than what is touted as the best way for a "love connection." Loving must first begin with loving God. According to the Bible, the truth is, God is love and in order to love, find love, and be loved, one must know and accept the love of God. First John 4:16 says, *"And we have known and believed the love that God hath to us. God is love; and he that dwelleth in love dwelleth in God, and God in him."* In this scripture, the word love comes from a Greek word, agápē, and is translated charity, which means benevolent love. According to the Hebrew-Greek Study Bible's definition of agape, this love is not shown by doing what the person loved desires but what the one who loves deems as needed by the one loved. It is an unselfish love because it recognizes, appreciates and desires to fulfill the need of the one for whom the love is shown.

In His infinite wisdom, God knew that man needed such love. Because of the sinful state of a fallen world (due to the sin of Adam), God determined to demonstrate His love for us by sending His Son to die for our sins. It is impossible to articulate and comprehend such a great love. God's love for us was and is so great that He sacrificed His only Son in order that we might know love. It was an unselfish act for which a greater love has never been witnessed.

God's love transcends any of man's efforts to show and know love. His sacrifice on our behalf is without equal and can never be replicated. However, God's demonstration of love to us was given in order that we might receive it, internalize it (spiritually) and reciprocate it through a loving relationship with Him and with others. First John 4:19-21 says, *"We love him [God] because He first loved us. If a man say, I love God, and hateth his brother, he is a liar: for he that loveth not his brother whom he hath seen, how can he love God whom he hath not seen? And this commandment have we from him [God], That he who loveth God love his brother also.* This scripture tells us that we can love God because He loved us first — He demonstrated how to love unselfishly by sacrificing His Son. Once we accept His love, we are then free and ready to love others. We can show real love because we have seen love and accepted love from the Father, Who is Love.

Before we were married, my husband asked me why I loved him. Although I wanted to say exactly what he wanted me to say, I was unable to give him a specific answer. I assumed that because I had agreed to marry him, because he was a Christian, and because he had not shown evidence of behaviors that suggested that he was not a good person, he was worthy of my love. I therefore assumed that he understood that I loved him, knowing why was not a question I thought needed answering. I really never thought about "why" I loved him; I just did. I cannot remember the answer I gave him at the time. I was spiritually immature and my expression of love as a woman was very much based on my experiences from the world. My perception of finding 'Mr. Right' was based on many years of reading books and seeing movies filled with stories of romantic encounters involving a guy, a girl, a kiss, a proposal and living happily ever after as man and wife. I am sure that my answer to him was "politically correct" but I am also sure that I did not grasp the significance and the depth of his question. I better understood his question as we grew in marriage and after he died. While he was alive, our love for one another grew stronger as we were facing the trials and tribulations of marriage. As a young couple we were trying to make ends meet, struggling to appreciate each other's imperfections, and in the last two years of marriage, dealing with a health challenge that would ultimately cause his death.

After Steve died, I realized that while I had experienced romantic love in marriage, I had also been the recipient of real love, agapé love, and had the opportunity to show real love. This love superseded our perceptions of romantic love and was the foundation and the "glue" that kept us together as we went through the trials and difficulties that are often a part of marriage.

The love I felt for my husband was and is unexplainable, yet real and rewarding. Real love is indescribable yet simply identifiable. It is agapé — a tangible demonstration of love from God — Spirit love, without condition or measure. One writer suggests that this is love that is defined by God's action in sending Jesus Christ into the world. It was love that reached out to those who did not deserve it; a love that put the interest of others first, a love that forgave people and started over with them; and a love that sacrificed itself for others. It is that caring, forgiving, spontaneous, redeeming love which is the essence of God's nature. This is the love that is the key to living.

The significance and essentiality of this Pearl is found in 1 Corinthians 13. This chapter of the Bible is known as the "love chapter" because it very clearly and specifically tells us why love is the key to living. In this chapter, the word "charity" is used for the word love. The chapter begins by indicating the supremacy of love. It is supreme over all possessions, abilities, knowledge, and even faith. In other words, love is essential for any aspect of our lives and living to have value and worth.

The chapter goes on to indicate the attributes and actions of love. It suggests that love has to become the response to treatment by others. When we are treated kindly, we must respond with love. We must also respond with love when we are not treated kindly. As a matter of fact, 1 Corinthians 13:4 tells us that love suffers long and with the suffering, it remains kind. This means that love has what one writer calls an infinite capacity for endurance and patience. Love has great patience toward evil and it shows goodness towards those who ill-treat it. Love is the response that endures even when presented with treatment that is unkind, unwarranted and undeserved.

I know that it sounds rather trite to say that no matter how we are treated, we must respond with love. The question that arises is, how? When we consider the difficulties, tragedies and misfortunes that daily plague our lives, how do we respond with the attributes and actions of love?

I believe the answer to this question is found in a statement Jesus made to the

disciples. On the evening before He was crucified, Jesus shared the Passover meal with
the disciples. That evening, there were many
things said but I believe John 15:12 gives
us the simple answer to the question of how
to respond with love at all times and in all
circumstances. Jesus said, "*This is my commandment, That ye love one another, as I have
loved you.*"

There are three aspects of Jesus' statement to the disciples that give us direction in
having a love response. First, Jesus told the
disciples that loving one another was "His"
commandment. In this instance, the word
commandment means instruction. In other
words, Jesus gave the disciples instructions
to love — they really had no other choice if
they were to continue to live lives that were
pleasing to God. He had demonstrated this
instruction during the three years of His
earthly ministry. He demonstrated it by loving
when the religious leaders of that day publicly
humiliated and ridiculed Him. He demonstrated the instructions by loving when His
credibility was questioned, even by His own
family. As Jesus *was* the living example to
the disciples of how to respond with love,
He *is* the living example of how to respond
with love for us. We can respond with love no
matter how we have been treated because the
love response is a commandment. It is what
Jesus has instructed us to do. As Jesus is
the One who is the only unquestionable and

undeniable demonstration of the Love of God, we must follow His instruction.

The second aspect of Jesus' statement to the disciples that helps us understand how to respond with love is His instruction to love "one another." For many years as a Christian, I always understood this statement to mean that I should love everybody. In an effort to help our congregation to see the significance of loving one another, my pastor preached that we have to love everyone; including those who seem to be unlovable and unlovely. As much as this is what the Bible says and as much as I tried to do it, I have to admit that I have not always been able to love "everybody." There have been times in my life where I have experienced racial hatred, rejection, disillusionment and other offenses that left me struggling to present the proper Christian love response. Thankfully, as I have grown as a Christian, loving according to Christ's instructions has become more readily attainable. The lens through which I view offenses, mistreatment, and perceived hurts has been changed so that I have a clearer view of myself and others. A more consistent examination and purging of the unlovely attitudes and actions that were a part of my life and living helped me to change the lens. This is what I believe Jesus meant in Matthew 7:1-5. In this passage of scripture, Jesus cautions that we not find fault with or condemn others. For the Christian, attention to human imperfection in others while being unable to see one's own shortcomings and sins is hypocritical. When we experience offenses and hurts, it is very easy to accuse and criticize others. What Jesus requires is mercy and forgiveness as aspects of love.

Many years ago, I heard Pastor Dewey Lane say that loving one another can be easier understood and accomplished if we considered it as a commandment to "love one and then another." I believe he meant that one should view each opportunity to show God's love with a singular focus. That is, the person to whom the love is given should be considered for his or her uniqueness and the uniqueness of the need for love. Once we have examined ourselves to correct the unlovely things that cause us to view others as unlovely, we can then focus on loving one person and then another and another and another and another, until ultimately, we will find ourselves loving "everybody."

The third aspect of Jesus' commandment that helps us to see how to respond in love is the last five words — "as I have loved you." I believe there is such an intimacy of relationship reflected in these words to the disciples. Jesus' final instructions to the disciples reveal His desire to help them deal with the fact that their leader, counselor and friend was about to leave them. For some time, He had tried to assure them of the necessity of the crucifixion and the triumph of the resurrection. Now, He was trying to prepare them to carry on the ministry He had started. The instruction to love in the same way He loved was necessary to remind them of the sacrificial and unconditional nature of His love. This would be essential to their lives after the resurrection because they would face persecution, ridicule and even hatred from those whom they would serve. Loving as He had loved them would allow them to consider their ways and realize that even when they were unlovable, He loved them.

Responding with love is made simple when we remember the love that God has shown us through the life, death, burial and resurrection of Jesus Christ. He is our Saviour and He has given us specific instructions to love sacrificially and unconditionally whenever and wherever possible. We can do it because He told us to and because He loved us when we did not want His love or deserve it.

According to 1 Corinthians 13:8 "*Love never fails [never fades out or becomes obsolete or comes to an end]* " (Amplified Version). Because love never fails, it is essential and effective for living. The rest of this verse lists things that will eventually fail. In essence, whatever may be acquired, learned, or experienced in this life is temporary. Love is the only thing that will exist into eternity because God is love and love is God. The key to living is loving means that in order to live, that is have real life, fulfilling and overflowing, one must love — know and give the love of God.

The Key to Living is Loving!

Chapter Three

Pearl Two:
The Key to Loving is Giving!

For God so loved the world, that he gave his only begotten Son, that whosoever believeth in Him should not perish, but have everlasting life. For God sent not his Son into the world to condemn the world; but that the world through him might be saved (John 3:16-17).

I cannot say that my husband had the spiritual gift of giving but what I know with certainty is that he was a ceaseless giver of his time and attention. I have never met anyone who was more giving of themselves with respect to time and attention as my husband. His ability to "tune in" the person with whom he was communicating and his ability to "tune out" any distraction that could easily destroy the "undivided attention" necessary for the moment was impeccable. In this, I saw the love of God manifested in his life time and time again.

When we met, I did not know that he was paying attention to me. I learned years after we were married that he pursued me with a vengeance. From the day we met, he was willing to give of himself in an effort to demonstrate his love for me. It was not tangible items, trinkets or gifts that he gave; it was his time and attention out of a heart of love for God and for me. His giving was more than an act; it was a reflection of God's love.

The act of giving is evident throughout society. For some, giving is considered a selfless act. Our headlines are replete with stories of large tips being given to servers in restaurants and money being given to strangers in need. Billionaires, millionaires and even the average nine-to-fiver find a sense of "goodness" in giving money to a cause. Great lengths are taken to advertise and fundraise for causes that involve a myriad of societal problems, diseases and symptoms. Many of these efforts have raised millions of dollars for providing research that will one day help find the cure for cancer. Other efforts have provided resources and aid for people whose families have been devastated by natural disasters. In these acts of giving, the giver identifies what is presented as a need and shares out of his or her substance. In many instances, the giver and the receiver are both grateful and blessed to be engaged in the act of giving.

The Key to Loving is Giving is a Pearl that suggests giving that not only flows out of a desire to meet a need with one's substance, it is about giving that is essential because of love. With this giving, a need may or may not be present or understood and money may or may not be involved. This is giving prompted by love (the love of God) and expressed because of that love.

As the scripture reference for this Pearl says, God loved us so much that He gave His only begotten Son to die for our sins. His love compelled Him to give so that we could know Him, love Him, please Him and serve Him because He is the only true and living God. In essence, God's love was given so that we could have an intentional, purposeful and exclusive relationship with Him.

Based on God's example, the key to loving is giving because love compels one to give. To compel means to drive or urge forcefully or irresistibly. When we accept love from God and His love is in our hearts, we are irresistibly driven to give. God's love is powerful and when the power of God's love is in us, we cannot help but give what we have been given. His love drives and urges us to give love.

Giving in this context is not philanthropy. This kind of giving is often chosen to make one feel better or safer because of what is hoped for with the giving. In many instances, philanthropic giving emanates from a logical mindful decision with an expectation that certain results will occur. When this is the case, giving begins with a monetary or material commitment and ends when there are no more causes or no more money. While philanthropic giving is necessary, important and a welcomed aspect of our daily lives, the focus of this Pearl is giving that originates from the heart of God and finds its expression in the heart of man.

For the Christian, giving begins with a heart that is committed to loving God because He first loved us. In his second letter to the church at Corinth, the Apostle Paul explains how faithful the Macedonian church had been in their giving. While the church did not have great wealth, they were consistent in giving resources to the Apostle Paul for the work of ministry. They were commended for giving resources; however, in 2 Corinthians 8:5, Paul says that before the members of the Macedonian church gave resources, they *"first gave their own selves to the Lord."* That we first give ourselves to the Lord is the core of this Pearl. God's love for us compelled Him to give His Son. Giving one's self to the Lord begins with accepting Jesus Christ as Saviour and continues as we grow and develop in relationship with Him. Once we give ourselves to the Lord, giving becomes an integral, undeniable and inseparable part of who we are. We are compelled through love to give our time, our gifts and talents, and our treasure.

Love compels us to give of what might be considered the most precious commodity of the age - time. Whether we realize it or not, time has been given to us by God. Through His mercy, He has set the world and all things necessary for life in place so that we could live within the boundaries of space and time. Each day that the sun rises, we all have an equal measure of the gift of time. Twenty-four hours is given to every man, woman, boy and girl all over the world. How we use the gift of time is completely left up to us. Interestingly, God gave it, He controls it, and He has the final say as to when there will be no more of it; however, He does not force us to give any of it to Him. Rather, by giving us His love, He desires that we will respond to love by giving Him our time.

In order to understand giving time, it is important to pair the word time with the word attention. Whereas time is the gift God has given us, attention is the application of our mental and emotional faculties with the time. God gives us time and we give time our attention.

To me, my husband was the consummate giver of time and attention. Even years after his passing, people who knew him often speak of his ability to make them feel as if they were the only persons to whom such considerate and personal attention was given. Whether meeting him casually on the street or sitting across from him at a counseling table, they speak of his extraordinary ability to make them feel as if theirs was the only situation or conversation of importance or significance at that time. His giving made them feel loved because he gave them time and attention.

Time and attention are inseparable. In our busy lives, we are often able to give one at a time but, in a world of information overload, we are often unable to effectively give both. When the love of God is in our hearts, we should give both. This is especially true as it relates to the time and attention needed in our relationship with the Lord. It is the time and attention that we give to the relationship with the Lord that helps us and matures us so that we can give time and attention to others.

I have been guilty of not giving time and attention to the Lord as I should. Even as a preacher and full-time staff person for my church, there have been times when the business of ministry and the whirlwind of life have caused me to "skimp" on personal time and attention in my relationship with the Lord. Sometimes it is easy to give Him time — those few minutes of prayer that precede the calendar full of appointments and meetings that I want to go well. What is missing is attention — the focus on what He wants to say to me after I have said what I want to say to Him. In these instances, time is not enough, attention must be given so that I have an uncluttered mind, a proper focus, and a spirit that is in tune with the Spirit of God. This can only be done as I bring my thoughts into captivity (2 Corinthians 10:5), unplug my emotions, and detach from the noise of the day. When we give God time and attention, the result is a mind that is more God-centered than problem- and situation-centered. When our minds are God-centered, we are better equipped to give others time and attention.

Our gifts and talents are also a very significant part of giving. As is the case with time, gifts and talents are given to us from God. They are the spiritual tools we need so that, as part of the Body of Christ, we are able to function, be protected and be mature. Our gifts and talents serve as a type of "glue" that bonds us together.

The importance of giving spiritual gifts is found in Romans 12, which tells us that the Body of Christ is one Body with many members. Each member has been given spiritual gifts and they are given from God by the Holy Spirit. They enable the entire Body of Christ to function as a unit. With these gifts, according to 1 Corinthians 12, each member is to give his or her gift through service. No matter where or how the gift is given, whether in places of high visibility or low visibility, no one gift is more significant or necessary than another. Each member has an important purpose. Not even one's past condition or current situations and circumstances can destroy the significance, importance and necessity of the gift that must be given as a part of the Body of Christ.

Our talents are like the special features of our being that make us who we are. They are necessary in conjunction with spiritual gifts to make the Body appealing, enjoyable, and engaging. Our talents should be given out of a heart of gratitude for God. In His infinite wisdom, He determined to make each of us unique through natural talents.

Whenever I use the word talent, I am reminded of something that happened when I was about 12 years old. We lived in a neighborhood that was not middle class and not quite poor. My street was sandwiched between what was known as the "projects." Around the corner from my house to the left and to the right were rows of houses that were known as welfare houses. I had friends in the houses around each corner. Other than the name given, I was not clear on the difference between them and me. I just didn't live in the projects.

Whether considered regular houses or welfare houses, in my estimation my neighborhood (projects included) had some great talent. There were the girls that could jump rope way better than I could. Double Dutch was usually the game of the day and anyone with real skill didn't even think about "jumping in" unless your feet were fast and light. There were my brother's friends who could pitch and hit a softball better than anyone I knew. They learned from the best as we spent many summer afternoons at RFK Stadium watching the Washington Senators play ball. While I did not have friends that could sing (I certainly couldn't), most, if not all of my friends could dance. I mean really dance. We could do every one of the Supremes' steps, the Temptations had nothing on us, and we could even imitate James Brown sliding across living room linoleum. In case any of those names are not familiar to you, suffice it to say that they were the singing and dancing celebrities of my day. With our precise and well-put together imitations of their fancy footwork, I thought we were a pretty talented bunch.

One day, the neighborhood was abuzz because there was a man going door to door with an accordion. Word on the street was that he was going throughout the neighborhood to find children with talent. We lived two houses from the corner and by the time the man with the accordion reached our house, news of the search had spread to the homes at the opposite end of the block. Since I was the oldest child, I was selected as the test case. My parents allowed him to give me the accordion and he began the "test" to see if I had talent. I vaguely remember the noise from the accordion and snickers from my brothers and sisters as I attempted to play. I was nervous because I did not think I had talent but I wanted to see if anyone else thought I did.

I do not remember the outcome of the talent search. My parents never told me. What I do remember is my friends teasing me for days saying, "you don't have no talent." I was crushed and vowed to never think or act as if I had something of value to offer. If the man who was looking for talent did not think I had talent and if my friends and family did not think I had talent, I did not have talent.

Thankfully, I grew to understand that talent is not something that is verified by the eyes and ears of others. I also learned that everyone has talent. Even those who think they do not have it are endowed with abilities that make them unique yet essential to the world around them. That is what talent is; it is God-given, unique to the one who has it, and given for the purpose of sharing it. Psalms 139:14 says that we are fearfully and wonderfully made, a marvelous work of the Lord's hands. One writer translates this verse to say, "Lord, you are awesome and with wonders I have been distinguished because Your workmanship is marvelous." Each human being is a distinguished and marvelous creation of God. No matter how we see ourselves, there are distinguishing features of our existence that have been engraved into our very being. This, I believe is what talent is. It is God-designed, God-breathed and God-appointed.

Out of His great love, God has graciously given us time, gifts and talents. As His love compelled Him to give, the key to loving is giving our time, gifts and talents as a demonstration of love. We demonstrate that we have received the love of God in our hearts when we give our time, gifts and talents.

Giving of our treasure is equally as important as giving of our time and talents. The Bible says that where our treasure is there is also our heart (Matthew 6:21). This scripture suggests a connection between our treasure, both spiritual and natural and what is in our hearts.

Giving of our treasure means giving of natural and material things we have been given. Actually, what we have that is natural like money, housing, food, etc. is given because of God's love. While the Lord does not have these things in Heaven, the Bible says that the cattle on a thousand hills belong to the Lord. Therefore, no matter what we possess, it is because God is merciful that we have it. This is further understood in Psalm 24:1which says, "The earth is the Lord's, and the fullness thereof; the world, and they that dwell therein." Because of His infinite mercy, God has determined to orchestrate the pages of time in a manner that the earth, its inhabitants, and all of the galaxies beyond the earth move and turn at just the right speed and tenure so that we can enjoy and experience one day at a time. Although we live in a world that is laden with sin, our existence depends on God's mercy; His compassion that causes

Him to hold all things together until the final judgment when Christ returns.

Lamentations 3:22 says that is of the Lord's mercy that we are not consumed. This means that because God is merciful, the world as we know it is held together in a way that every day, nature and natural forces like gravity and the laws of aerodynamics function in a way that allows the universe to cooperate so that we go about living. The "brand new mercy" is ours every day. This is how we can enjoy the world in which we live. What we possess is a direct result of God's mercy. Without it, there would be no world in which to live; God is the Creator and the Sustainer of all that we see and experience. Because He is merciful, we have natural treasure.

Treasure is the natural substance or material we possess. In Matthew 6:19-21, the Bible tells us that we should not focus on storing up or accumulating natural or material things. It is obvious in today's society that getting, keeping and maintaining things has become an essential aspect of life. We are ardent consumers. In recent years, the extent to which consumerism and materialism have overshadowed our daily living is evident as many people engage in hoarding behavior. This verse of scripture tells us that things can become worthless, wear out, or be stolen.

What Jesus said in these verses is that there is a better kind of treasure and a safer place in which to keep that treasure. The kind of treasure Jesus spoke of is the treasure of the heart or one's affections and desires that result from knowing the love of God and having a desire to please Him. The place where this treasure is secure is Heaven. Jesus told His followers to store up or accumulate an affection and desire to do the will of the Father so that the Heavenly account would be full of acts of love and kindness that please God. Thus, the Heavenly account is reflected in that same love and kindness toward man.

In Acts 20:35, the Apostle Paul addresses the church at Ephesus concerning giving. He uses himself as an example by saying that he had worked or labored with his hands. Paul was a tent maker and although he preached throughout the known world, during his ministry he also worked in order to support himself and in order to give into the work of ministry. In verse 35, Paul admonishes the believers at Ephesus to do the same thing. They were encouraged to work hard so that they could give to those who were weak and in need. He also admonished the church in Ephesians 4:28 to stop stealing (pilfering as a way of life) and work hard so that they would have to give.

The Word of God is clear with respect to what we must do with natural treasure. We should not focus on storing it up. This does not mean that we cannot have wealth; rather, wealth and an abundance of natural things must not be the focus of one's existence.

Natural treasure, once gained through honest and hard work, should be shared with those who are weak and in need. When we do this, the use of our natural treasure reflects the presence of great spiritual treasure that is pleasing to God and of great value that will not corrupt or tarnish.

The Key to Loving is Giving!

Chapter Four

Pearl Three:
The Roadblock to Giving is the Protection of Self!

But this I say, He which soweth sparingly shall reap also sparingly; and he which soweth bountifully shall reap also bountifully. Every man according as he purposeth in his heart, so let him give; not grudgingly, or of necessity: for God loveth a cheerful giver. And God is able to make all grace abound toward you; that ye, always having all sufficiency in all things, may abound to every good work (2 Corinthians 9:6-8).

As loving requires giving, giving requires an openness and a freedom that can only be found in unselfishness. It requires selflessness. I know that the idea of being selfless, that is, not considering or protecting self is very hard to grasp in the world in which we live. Selfishness is an aspect of protecting oneself. A person who is selfish is one who is concerned excessively and/or exclusively with self. To be selfish means to seek or concentrate on one's own advantage, pleasure or well-being without regard for others. The definition and description of selfishness seem hard because typically, no one wants to admit or own up to self-centeredness. To help us out in this dilemma, from a natural perspective, we were all born with the tendency to be selfish. We were born with what some consider survival instincts called reflexes. Researchers suggest that reflexes are the newborn's most obvious patterns of behavior. These reflexes cannot be taught but are necessary for the newborn to thrive and survive. Sucking is one of these reflexes.

What is interesting about this instinctual aspect of human life is that as an infant develops, he or she adapts certain reflex actions to new and varying conditions in the environment. In the womb, an unborn child can be seen exhibiting reflexive behavior. While many reflexes start in the womb, they are the beginning of more complex and purposeful behaviors. As the baby grows, reflexes "drop out" because they are not used as much. As we grow from birth into adulthood, what began as an instinct (reflex) to protect the self is replaced with behaviors that become a part of human life. The reason certain reflexes "drop out" at certain points in development is that they are used less and less. Since they are rarely used, they are therefore replaced with purposeful behavior.

I remember watching my nieces and nephews grow beyond breastfeeding to taking a bottle and on to the infamous pacifier. As they grew into toddlers, the goal was to wean them from the bottle and the pacifier. The expectation for each child was that ultimately, he or she would be able to self feed and not need assistance. This milestone of growth and development required a series of weaning practices like hiding the pacifier, spelling its name when the child was obviously looking for it, or giving it a name like "binky" and saying that it, along with the bottle, had gone "bye bye." These efforts were meant to soothe a reflex in hopes that a new behavior like drinking from a cup would develop. I can remember family cheers when one of my nieces or nephews started using a Sippy cup and did not want the "binky" any longer. The purposeful behavior of drinking from a cup was an indication of growth for the child. As an added benefit, there would no longer be a need to find, hide or buy a new binky.

While the scientific explanation of inborn self-directed behavior gives us somewhat of a "pass" on having just a bit of selfishness as a part of our make-up, a key point in the science is that ultimately, instinct must give way to purposeful behavior. This is what Pearl Three addresses and it is necessary in the life of the Christian. When we become Christians, there are natural instincts like reflexes that are a part of our former lives. We instinctively gave way to the lust of the flesh, the lust of the eyes, and the pride of life (I John 2:15-17). Much like an infant, we instantaneously did what was necessary to protect ourselves so that we could thrive in sinful habits and attitudes. However, just as an infant grows away from reflexes to function with purposeful behavior, we should allow the old instincts of *selfishness* to be replaced with a new purposeful behavior of *selflessness*.

It is necessary to recognize and address selfishness as a threat to one's ability to give and ultimately love according to God's plan. Because the key to loving is giving and because God so beautifully and specifically showed this truth to us, it is imperative that we remove selfishness as a roadblock to living and loving according to the will of God. While selfishness may be a natural tendency, it is not limited to certain actions. If we continue in it, selfishness becomes more than acts of withholding things from others. The danger is that it can escalate from being a seemingly insignificant natural tendency to a well-developed and rigid way of thinking. It can become a stronghold or what my pastor describes as a fortified opinion against the truth. Once a natural tendency develops into a way of thinking that presents selfish desires over the truth of God's Word, a stronghold is developed and it must be pulled down immediately and effectively (2 Corinthians 10:4-6). Strongholds "fuel" or give strength to selfish thoughts and selfish thoughts are manifested in selfish attitudes that perpetuate selfish actions. This cannot continue in our lives if we are to effectively use and appreciate the key to loving which is giving.

The opposite of selfishness is unselfishness. Since we are born with a natural tendency to be selfish, how do we stop it? This question gives way to another question. If my selfish tendency has developed into strongholds or fortified opinions against the truth, how can something so deeply rooted in my thoughts and actions be changed? The answer is, we need help. It is impossible to manage and maintain a completely selfless approach to life when we are clothed in flesh that is instinctively drawn to self preservation and gratification. Just as infants need help to grow into toddlers and toddlers need help to develop into children and so on, we need help to grow into mature Christians who live, love and give according to God's plan.

That is the beauty of what God has done in sending His Son to die for our sins. Because of love (beyond our understanding or worthiness to receive), He gave what we would need in order to mortify the deeds of the flesh and pull down the strongholds that are the result of instinctive or natural reflexes. Jesus told the disciples when He was about to ascend to the throne of God, after His resurrection, that they would be responsible for sharing and demonstrating the same love that He had shared with them from the Father. He also told them that, in order to carry out the assignment that He had given them, they would need power or help that only He could supply (Mark 16:9-20, Luke 24:46-49). The help they needed was given to them through the infilling of the Spirit of God - the Holy Spirit.

In order to change from being selfish to living unselfishly, we must allow the love of God which is given to us through Jesus Christ to take absolute control of our lives. In Ezekiel 36:22-27, a prophecy is given to the nation of Israel concerning its future status with the Lord. While the prophecy was given to Israel, it includes a statement that speaks to the status of those who have accepted Jesus Christ as Lord and Saviour. The Lord told Ezekiel to prophesy that the time would come when He would put His Spirit, the Holy Spirit, in man causing him to walk in His statutes or standards and causing him to keep His judgments or commands.

As the Lord spoke through the prophet Ezekiel and as Jesus shared with the disciples, in order to do the will of God, we have to have help. In order to shed the pull and the limiting constraint of selfishness and to become unselfish in our thoughts and actions, we need the power of the Holy Spirit to help us. It is the power of God through the work of the Holy Spirit that enables us to overcome the daily pull of the flesh that causes us to try to please, support and ultimately protect the flesh.

In the scripture reference for this Pearl, 2 Corinthians 9:6-8, the Apostle Paul is speaking to the church at Corinth. This second letter was written in part to commend the church for heeding instructions from the first letter and in chapter nine, he provides instruction and encouragement with respect to giving. He speaks to them concerning how to give - with the right attitude and heart condition. He also speaks to them about the results of giving — manifestation of the love God, an unceasing measure of the Grace of God, and the ability to be involved in the works of God. In essence, he graciously and tactfully admonishes the believers not to be selfish in their giving.

The Apostle Paul's encouragement to the believers at Corinth suggests three things that can be done in order to remove the road-block to Godly and effective giving. To change from selfishness that blocks giving to unself-ishness that opens the way to experiencing the love, grace and works of God, one must first **decide** not to be selfish. In 2 Corinthians 9:7, Paul tells the church to give according to how they "purposeth" in their hearts. The word purposeth means a conscious decision made after thought. In other words, after an examination of my thoughts to identify any selfishness, a decision must be made. To not be selfish, we must make a conscious decision to replace our selfish thoughts with an unselfish attitude

Indeed, selfishness (protection of self) is a part of our natural makeup. The newborn's instinctive reflex to automatically suckle to receive nourishment provides an example of how effortlessly we work toward protecting and maintaining the flesh. Just as the newborn's elementary reflexes are gradually replaced with purposeful behaviors as the environment and its demands require it, to rid ourselves of the negative influence of selfishness, we must allow our new life in Christ Jesus to help us to mortify the deeds of the flesh. Then, we can live a life characterized by unselfish behaviors and attitudes.

Romans 8:12-13 says, *"Therefore, brethren, we are debtors, not to the flesh, to live after the flesh. For if ye live after the flesh, ye shall die: but if ye through the Spirit do mortify the deeds of the body, ye shall live."* The first part of this verse of scripture helps us to see that we are not "in debt" to the flesh to continue to exhibit the ungodly reflexes that are inherent in our un-regenerated flesh. We owe nothing to the flesh and are therefore not obligated to be selfish. That's right, we do not have to be selfish. The second part of the verse gives us an additional key to ridding ourselves of selfishness: mortify the deeds of the flesh. One interpretation of this verse reads, "through being under the sway of the Spirit, you are putting your old bodily habits to death." [5]

The second thing we must so in order to get rid of selfishness as a roadblock to giving is to **determine** to know that God loves an unselfish heart. Second Corinthians 9:7 says that God loves a cheerful giver. Many Christians do not know that because God gave, He expects and requires that we give. While the giving that Paul refers to in this book of the Bible has to do specifically with monetary giving, the significance to living this Pearl is to understand that giving for the Christian involves far more than money and things. God is a Spirit and His desire for us is to give out of the love that He has so freely and magnificently given.

When verse 7 says that God loves a cheerful giver, it is necessary to understand that the word love in this context is the Greek word agapáō, a variation of the word agápē. Its meaning differs in this context. Here, the word agape means to find joy. In other words, God finds joy in us or we fulfill God's joy when we are unselfish and give out of the gifts and talents He has given us. We also fulfill God's joy when we give our time in service to others. In Matthew 10, Jesus chose and sent forth the twelve Apostles to serve and preach. As they were sent out, they were not to profit monetarily from their service. Jesus had given them power to heal the sick, cleanse the lepers, raise the dead and cast out demons. In Matthew 10:8, Jesus said, "freely ye have received, freely give." Knowing that God's joy is fulfilled when we give should help and enable us to live unselfishly in every area of our lives.

The third thing we must do in order to rid ourselves of selfishness is to **demonstrate** the decision and the determination to change selfish behaviors and attitudes. This is done by doing all that we do without concern for our own needs and without a motivation to receive.

Second Corinthians 9:8 tells us what happens when we decide, determine and then demonstrate that we have removed selfishness as the roadblock to giving. Verse eight in the Amplified Bible reads, *"And God is able to make all grace (every favor and earthly blessing) come to you in abundance, so that you may always and under all circumstances and whatever the need be self sufficient [possessing enough to require no aid or support and furnished in abundance for every good work and charitable donation].* The verse begins with the words "God is able," which means that removing selfishness as a roadblock to giving allows God to do a work in us and with us so that our lives are absolutely controlled and influenced by His presence. We live knowing that His hand is on our lives. In other words, we experience real relationship with God. As you will see throughout the pages of this book, it is this wonderful and incomprehensible relationship with the Lord that so beautifully gives us real life and strength for living daily.

By ridding ourselves of selfishness, God is able. He is able or allowed to bring to pass seven things in our lives according to verse 8 and the remaining verses of 2 Corinthians 9. When we mortify the deeds of the flesh and live unselfishly, the following seven things happen:

1. *Our righteousness remains forever* - the testimony of my unselfish living casts an indelible, irreversible and everlasting imprint in the sphere of influence in which I live. When I live an unselfish life, God's love is made more visible and His work in me is made more desirable. This is why this book is being written.

2. *Our seed is multiplied and fruit of my righteousness increases* - here, the Apostle Paul prays that the unselfish giver would know that God is the Source of all that we have. He also prays that God would multiply our store of seed. This means that as more of God's Word is received and applied in our lives, our hearts become a storehouse for it. As our store of seed is multiplied, opportunities for the righteous deed of giving are multiplied. God's purpose is that as

we receive the Word, we become givers of the Word in our words and actions so that the fruit of righteousness would increase in our lives.

3. *We are enriched* - this action is in concert with the previous portion of the scripture. When I am unselfish in attitude and behavior and the Lord provides naturally and spiritually, I am enriched or wealthy (rich) as evidenced by how God works in my life.

4. *God is glorified* - when I am enriched, my life becomes an example that causes thanksgiving to God from me and those who witness His goodness in my life. Then, God is glorified.

5. *The needs of others will be supplied* - once I am unselfish in my actions and attitude, it is almost inevitable that others benefit from my life and lifestyle.

6. *We become witnesses of the goodness of God* - the giver's obedience to giving according to the Gospel of Jesus Christ allows him or her to be an "eyewitness" of the goodness of God. In other words, giving out of an unselfish heart allows the giver to experience the goodness of God firsthand.

7. *Our witness produces more witnesses* - as others are influenced by the testimony of God's goodness in our lives, they are encouraged to trust and believe

God to produce the same goodness in their lives.

I can remember my grandmother instructing us on the importance of giving and how not to be selfish. She would put coins in a handkerchief and tie it real tight so that she did not lose them. Occasionally, she would carefully open the handkerchief and give me and my siblings change to buy candy. Once the coins left the handkerchief and were placed in my hand, I would make a tight fist around them so that I could make it to the corner store to buy squirrel nuts, bubble gum or some other penny candy. Buying penny candy meant that my coins would go further and I would have candy for more than a day. Usually, before I could get out of the house and around the corner, one of my siblings would ask for some of "my" money. Typically, great chatter would go back and forth as they pleaded and I continually said "no!" Hearing the exchange between me and my siblings, my grandmother would say, "if you hold your hand so tight that nothing can get out, it won't be open for something else to come in." She was teaching me and my siblings about giving and selfishness. I believe she was saying that we cannot give and be selfish at the same time. If we are selfless enough to give, it opens up the possibility and opportunity for us to receive so that we can give again.

In order to give, selfishness has to be removed. What I have learned is that I must allow the power of God through the inspiration and direction of the Holy Spirit to show me how to move the roadblocks that selfishness creates. I admit that there are strongholds that I continue to work at pulling down. I have made many mistakes while trying to protect myself by trying to hold on to attitudes, thoughts and opinions that do not allow the truth of God's Word to come into my heart. But, I am so grateful for this Pearl. I am committed to deciding not to be selfish and determining to know that God loves an unselfish heart. My prayer is that with each opportunity to give according to the will of the Father, I am demonstrating my decision and determination.

Living, loving and giving are essential to and inseparable from the Christian life. Effectively dealing with the damage that selfishness can do in our lives is hard work, but it must be done. No matter how strong the pull of natural tendencies on our attitudes and actions, we must allow the power of the Holy Spirit to help us and to change us!

The Roadblock to Giving is the Protection of Self!

Chapter Five

Pearl Four:
The Key to Fulfillment is Found in the Smile of Another!

A merry heart maketh a cheerful countenance: but by sorrow of the heart the spirit is broken (Proverbs 15:13).

My father and my husband had similar smiles. Growing up as the oldest of my siblings, I enjoyed and took pride in seeing my father smile. I enjoyed it because along with his smile there was often a hearty laugh and the words, "that's beautiful baby." As a little girl, he made me feel like a princess. From what I understand, when I was born his father instructed him to never spank me and he never did. While he never spanked me, I always knew and understood his strength and authority as a father. I respected and revered my father's parental authority and leadership so much so that just a quick glance suggesting that my actions were less than pleasing to him caused me to stop the unaccepted behavior and quickly find what was acceptable in his sight. His smile meant that he was pleased and I was accepted. I knew he loved me; he demonstrated that in his great care and commitment to being an excellent father. But, there was something about love accompanied by a winning smile that filled my heart and encouraged my soul.

My husband's smile spread a bit further across the face than my father's did; however, it too was a significant source of encouragement for me. As a wife, his smile meant that I had his undivided attention. I am sure that there were times when he smiled even though he was not necessarily purposefully engaged in the conversation; however, because my actions suggested I needed it and sometimes at my insistence, he sat down or stood before me, looked at me and smiled. I knew that his love for me was unquestionable, but when he smiled, at once I felt protected, appreciated, and cared for.

Both my husband's smile and my father's smile were important to and necessary for me. They displayed a heart full of love and care and in response, I was filled with desire and determination to do what was necessary to acquire that same smile over and over again.

What they gave me with a smile was a sense of purpose and being that caused me to be a better me. Their smiles made me happy.

Have you ever entered a restaurant or eatery where the server not only said, "how may I help you" but also added a sincere smile? Somehow a genuine smile suggests that the bearer is pleased to do what they are about to do for you. Not only that, the smile is deposited like a token that says you are about to receive fulfillment in your dining experience.

The Key to Fulfillment is Found in the Smile of Another is a Pearl for living happily with others by giving an intangible, voluntary action that costs nothing yet yields benefits that are priceless. According to Webster's Dictionary, a smile is a pleasant or encouraging appearance and to fulfill means to satisfy, which means to make happy.[6] A smile reflects a cheerful disposition and without much effort on the part of the bearer/wearer, it can be a source of immediate encouragement. When we give someone a smile bathed in the love of God, we experience the satisfaction of giving something that can change an ordinary moment into and extraordinary moment. With a well-intended smile, moments of sorrow and grief can be turned into moments of celebration and joy. When the love of God is in us and we are compelled to give, a seemingly small yet powerful way that we can give of our time and attention is to give a smile. When we reflect the love of God and the magnificent grace that His loves provides, an infectious and engaging process begins. Others see and receive our smiles and often reciprocate with the same.

The scripture reference for this Pearl, Proverbs 15:13, is simple and direct. It describes what a merry heart does — it "makes" a cheerful countenance. A merry heart is one that has the love of God in it. When we have a relationship with God through Jesus Christ, we have an inner Source of joy and peace that can be drawn from in any situation and at any time. Because the Source of joy and peace are within, we can reflect what is on the inside with a smile. This same thought is found in Proverbs 17:22 which says, *"A merry heart doeth good like a medicine: but a broken spirit drieth the bones."* In Proverbs 15:13, the word "cheerful" is the same word for the words "doeth good" in Proverbs 17:22. As translated from the Hebrew, the word cheerful in this scripture means to be good, well, beautiful, pleasant, lovely, and glad. In essence, a heart full of the love of God makes the face or countenance pleasant and well. A pleasant, well and beautiful face is one that has a smile on it. When the love of God is in our hearts, it should make us smile.

The second part of the scripture defines what happens when a heart is full of sorrow or sadness. Many people live lives that are riddled with sorrow. Their plans and dreams have been crushed or destroyed because of difficult times and hard to deal with circumstances and situations. Under the pressures of life challenges, they succumb to a sorrowful life. The past is painful and is a constant reminder of good that did not happen. The future is bleak because of the failure and difficulties of the past. Their present situation seems hopeless because they are sandwiched between past regrets and future disappointments. The sorrow that veils their lives reflects a spirit that is broken and without hope. They need hope and help that can lift the veil of sorrow and ignite a fire of joy and cheer. This is what the Lord does in the heart of one who will accept His love, live in His love and share His love with others — He gives hope and offers help through the power of the Holy Spirit. As we receive and apply the hope and help God gives, a heart that was once cold and hard can be warmed to become merry. A merry heart reflects a hopeful spirit in the form of a simple yet powerful smile.

I do not know how or when the happy face symbol began to have such popularity. With the digital age, it is possible to post a happy face with e-mails and other sources of communication. I especially like the happy face with teeth. The infectious influence of the happy face has been anchored in most of my written expressions of kindness and care. Over the years, I have developed a habit of drawing a happy face around my name when

I sign cards and letters. For me, the symbol of happiness is given as both a gesture of warm regards and a reminder to the recipient to receive the smile and reciprocate by smiling in return, even though I may not be present to see it.

Because smiling is a voluntary action, it requires an unselfish attitude as was described in the previous Pearl. Once we live through loving and giving, having removed the roadblock of selfishness through the power of the Holy Spirit, we can choose to smile showing forth the love of God that encourages others. When we reflect the love of God and the magnificent grace that His loves provides, an infectious and engaging process begins.

The key to fulfillment lies in the smile of another because our fulfillment or the satisfaction of knowing and giving the love of God is evident when we smile. A smile, willingly and cheerfully displayed is more often than not returned with a corresponding smile. This is an indication that the love of God has been successfully transmitted.

The smiles that my husband and father gave me were given out of love, a love for God and a love for me as a daughter and a wife. The smiles were fulfilling in that a simple gesture given out of love drew a response from me that reflected my push to do better and to be better because of the source of the smile.

I am smiling as this Pearl is being written. My hope is that you receive it. If for some reason life has not been kind and you are wrapped in a blanket of regret for the past and are lost in a sea of dread for what the future holds, I want to encourage you to smile - that's it, smile! As you smile, think about the fact that even though your experiences in the past and the uncertainty of your future have consistently weighed heavily on your mind - God loves you! Yes, He loves you and He wants you to have a merry heart. He wants you to have a heart full of His love, saturated with His peace, and bursting with His joy. With a merry heart, you can smile knowing that the God and Father who created you is well aware of your situation and He wants to help you and give you hope.

If you have never considered receiving His love, just decide to do it right now. Stop reading for a moment, close your eyes, sit quietly, and ask Him to save you with His love. Once you have asked, do not question what just happened. Accept it and continue to smile. The more you smile remembering this moment, the more you will sense the love of God through His Son - Jesus is Lord!

I hope that this simple yet powerful Pearl will continue to warm your heart and I pray that you will use the key to fulfillment and smile. It will open a door of your life that will give you a real sense of satisfaction as you share your smile with others. From now on, each smile that you receive when you have given one freely will warm your heart because you will have encouraged others with the love of God. Keep smiling!

The Key to Fulfillment is Found in the Smile of Another!

Chapter Six

Pearl Five:
The Key to Joy Lies in the Joy of Others!

And now come I to thee; and these things I speak in the world, that they might have my joy fulfilled in themselves (John 17:13).

arly on in my Christian experience, I learned a simple and encouraging praise song that includes the words, "this joy that I have, the world didn't give it to me, the world didn't give it and the world can't take it away." I love that song and enjoy sharing in moments of praise and worship where every person singing it seems to relish the thought of joy without end, without limits and without threat of loss.

I think most of us can recall moments where words spoken or actions taken created a sense of joy. I loved seeing my husband experience such joy. While he enjoyed the fellowship and fun of family activities and get-togethers, he was not big on social celebrations, or festive gatherings. What he really enjoyed and what seemed to bring joy to his heart was seeing the joy of Christmas. I believe the meaning of Christmas was deeply personal to him because of his love for the Saviour and his desire to please God. From a natural perspective, he absolutely enjoyed giving and seeing the joy and happiness of the receiver. It gave him joy. He once told me that growing up, his father made a big deal over Christmas and Christmas toys. As a result, he loved the giving and sharing that were inherent in the Christmas season.

While he loved giving and sharing during the Christmas season, he found it difficult to decide exactly what to get me for Christmas. This was probably because he thought I was picky. We were worlds apart in our likes and dislikes. He was not at all interested in clothing, decorating, art, and the like. Let's just say I was a bit particular about what I liked.

We spent a lot of time picking out gifts for family and friends and often agreed that we would not exchange gifts. I think we both tried to minimize the challenge of having to figure out what to get each other. One year during our Christmas shopping, he suggested that we go in different directions to pick up some last minute gifts. He instructed me to go into a store where I had been eyeing the deep discounts in the jewelry section. I was to tell the salesperson what I liked. His plan was to go into the store at another time to retrieve my Christmas gift. I followed instructions and gave the salesperson several choices. I kept my choices within our Christmas budget and left the store excited about what my husband was going to do.

I was not sure that my husband would choose to get my gift from the store where I made all of the beautiful selections. Because he liked the element of surprise, I started thinking that he might have sent me into one store to distract me from what he was really going to do. Even though I knew that he liked to surprise me, in the days leading up to Christmas I tried to get him to say something that would help to secure my "Christmas joy." He would not say a word!

On Christmas Day, my husband and I went to church and returned home to pack the car with the Christmas bounty we were going to share with our families. Before leaving for Christmas dinner and after having loaded the car, we decided to open the gifts we had bought for each other. I think I gave him an electronic chess set and some electronic device (like most men, he loved gadgets). I know that he gave me more than one gift but I started to get joyful when he pulled out a jewelry box. I carefully peeled off the wrapping paper and breathed really deeply before opening the box. I was elated to see a 14 carat gold charm for a charm bracelet that we bought during our vacation the year before. Steve had engraved the words "Love Steve" on the back of the charm and I was happy and impressed with his thoughtfulness in purchasing one of my selections from the jewelry store. He was happy, I was happy, and we both basked in the joy of Christmas.

While I thought my husband had spread his joy for Christmas, I was pleasantly surprised when we returned home from Christmas dinner with our families. We had brought the many gifts we had received into the house and were in the process of preparing for bed when Steve called me into the living room. He pretended to begin a brief sermon or exhortation in front of the fireplace. Before continuing in his exhortation, he said something like "Mrs. Wright, I think I forgot something." I had no idea of what he was trying to say or do. He looked at me with a great big smile, placed his hand behind a picture on the mantel and pulled out another jewelry box. I was in tears and I hadn't even opened the box. I tried with everything in me to contain myself. So much so, that he had to help me take the wrapping off the box. I opened the box to find a gold watch. I had been saying that I wanted to buy a gold watch one day. Steve had allowed me to get a gold charm bracelet by putting it in lay-away. I had said that I would do the same one day in order to get a gold watch. But here was the gold watch that I eyed during our Christmas shopping trip. I was speechless, surprised and way beyond happy.

I questioned how we could afford it but Steve told me that he wanted me to have it. I cried on and off the rest of the evening. What made me happy and what made me cry with tears of joy was not so much that I had the watch, it was knowing that my husband loved me so much that he "wanted me to have it" and that he received so much joy in giving it to me.

Of course, natural things and special moments do not supply the same joy that comes from having a real relationship with the Lord. At times when we are joyful because of what the moment or the experience brings, the problem is that the moment passes, the things decay, and even if we remember with great detail the moment, as I did with the gold watch, and the people involved, we can never recreate what we understood to be the "joy" of the moment.

This Pearl, The Key to Joy Lies in the Joy of Others, does not speak of a momentary and fleeting sense of joy. The joy referred to in this Pearl is as the praise song mentioned earlier suggests — joy without end, without limits and without fear of loss. The joy that I saw in my husband and that I have continuously known since his passing is Jesus' Joy.

Jesus' Joy is relationship. As we saw in Pearl Two, The Key to Loving is Giving because God loves us; He gave the best of Himself that we might have a loving relationship with Him. In John 17, after Jesus had eaten the Last Supper with the disciples and had given them insight on His death and resurrection, before they left the Upper Room He prayed. How magnificent it must have been to have the Saviour of the world to host a meal, honor the guests through serving them, and then allow them to be present as He speaks to His Father and their God. In John 17:13, Jesus says, *"And now come I to thee; and these things I speak in the world, that they might have my joy fulfilled in themselves."* In this verse of scripture, Jesus is talking to the Father but He lets us know that what He said in the conversation with the disciples concerning His death and resurrection were spoken so that those who received it would have joy fulfilled in them. He wanted His Joy — the relationship that would be established through His death and resurrection — to be our Joy. He wanted you and me to have the relationship that He had with the Father.

Jesus made His Joy evident in two aspects of His life and ministry. First, Jesus' Joy is evident in *His Resurrection*. **His resurrection secured the relationship we have with God the Father**. In John 13, Jesus speaks to the disciples during the Last Supper about His death. He let them know that He will not be with them long and that He wanted them to receive a new commandment to love one another. The disciples were uncertain and confused about where Jesus was going and questioned whether they could go with Him.

In John 14, Jesus responds to their confusion and questions by telling them that they need not be troubled about His departure because He was going to prepare a place for them and that His leaving would establish the Way to the Father. In John 14:20, Jesus says, *"At that day ye shall know that I am in my Father, and ye in me, and I in you."* He assured the disciples that His resurrection would establish an **eternal connection** between them and the Father. In John 14:28, Jesus tells the disciples that what He was about to do should cause them to rejoice. In other words, His joy was to be with the Father so that we could have that same joy — relationship with the Father through Jesus' resurrection.

Jesus' Joy is also evident through His resurrection in that it established an **eternal commitment** to intercession on our behalf. When Jesus returned to the Father, He took a position at the "Right Hand of God." In this position, Jesus as our High Priest makes intercession or prays for us continually. Hebrews 7:24 tells us that Jesus continues as our High Priest. He holds His priesthood unchangeably because He lives forever. Hebrews 7:25 in the Amplified version of the Bible says, *"Therefore He is able to save to the uttermost (completely, perfectly, finally, and for all time and eternity) those who come to God through Him, since He is always living to make petition to God and intercede with Him and intervene for them."*

Secondly, Jesus' Joy is evident through *His Residence.* **As His resurrection secured the relationship we have with the Father, His residence ensures the relationship.** Jesus told the disciples in John 14 that He would not leave them comfortless or without the same love and help that He had given them while He was on earth. It was obvious that the disciples were concerned and confused about His departure. I can imagine the fear and the discouragement they must have felt as they listened to Him describe what the next several days would be like. As I consider that evening, I am reminded of how unprepared I have been for the departures of my husband, my father and my mother. I was not with my husband when he departed and had no sense that the morning we sat in the bathroom talking would be the last day that he would be with me in our home. I was with my father from the day I took him to the doctor to receive the cancer diagnosis. From that day, until his departure, I wanted to be with him every day. I did not want to believe that he would leave me and I thought being with him was necessary in order to see what

God would do to keep him here. As he grew sicker and less like the vibrant man I loved and adored, I was never prepared for his departure. My mother's illness became evident shortly after my father died. She was heartbroken and continuously repeated the words, "I just can't believe that WC left me." I watched as she became weaker and more insistent on not taking care of herself. As we watched her go from needing help around the house to having to be placed in a nursing home, I knew that her departure was at hand; however, I was not prepared for the terrible sense of loss that I still sometimes feel when my mind allows her stern yet loving voice to be heard in my ear.

I just do not think it is possible to adequately prepare for the departure of someone you love and trust. I thank God for what Jesus did and what He said that evening as He spoke to the disciples. His words to them are the words that have allowed me to have joy after the painful departures in my life.

I believe that the difficulty of dealing with departure is perhaps an aspect of what the disciples were feeling that evening. What would they do and how could they prepare for the departure of the Teacher, Friend and Leader they had come to love, trust and obey? It was only three short years and the relationship was being cultivated in ways that they could never have imagined. But Jesus told them that is was necessary for Him to go. That evening in the Upper Room, He was preparing them by giving them an example of how to love and serve and by assuring them that He would not leave them without evidence and proof of His love and the love of the Father.

In John 14, Jesus promised the disciples that He would come to them and that He would manifest Himself to them. The Holy Spirit is the manifestation of Jesus Christ in the believer. Jesus takes up residence on the inside of every believer through the person of the Holy Spirit. That evening in the Upper Room, Jesus told the disciples that the Holy Spirit, or the Comforter, would come after He departed. The disciples were assured that the connection and the strength of relationship would be the same and even greater because of the presence and the power of the Holy Spirit, as He would reside in them and with them.

In John 14:26, Jesus' promise to the disciples was that the Holy Spirit would come and reside on the inside to do three things. First, the Holy Spirit is a teacher. The word teacher in this context of scripture is the Greek word "didasko" and it suggests three things with respect to the teacher. It suggests that the teacher is one who knows the student, who calculates the increase of the understanding of the student, and who aims to shape the will of the student.

As a Teacher, the Holy Spirit knows the one in whom He resides. Like Jesus, He knows us better than we know ourselves. Jesus demonstrated His knowing to the disciples on several occasions during His earthly ministry. In John 1 when Philip was trying to get Nathanael to become a disciple of Christ, he (Nathanael) made a snide remark about Jesus being from Nazareth. He had not seen Jesus nor had he met Him. As Nathanael approached Jesus, Jesus commented on Nathanael's character, letting him know that He knew him. Jesus went on to tell Nathanael that he saw him under a fig tree, which was an indication of His omniscient power. In a first acquaintance, Jesus the Teacher, let the disciple know that He knew him.

Throughout His ministry with the disciples, Jesus did what the Holy Spirit does as a Teacher on the inside of the believer. He showed them in several passages of scripture that He knew them to the point of knowing exactly what they were thinking. Like the Holy Spirit, Jesus also calculated the increase of their understanding. In other words, He knew when they were "getting it." In Matthew 16, Jesus had a conversation with Peter where He asked him a simple yet profound set of questions. Peter's answer to Jesus' question, "whom say ye that I am?" was "thou are the Christ, the Son of the living God." Jesus assured Peter that his answer had been revealed to him from God the Father.

As a result, Jesus called Peter blessed, that is, fully satisfied because he had heard from God. Certainly, the revelation from God to Peter served to strengthen the foundation of his faith and relationship with God.

Not only does the Holy Spirit reside on the inside of us as a Teacher who knows us and who calculates or determines the increase in our understanding, His goal is to shape our wills to do the will of the Father. This is Jesus' example to the disciples and it is His example to every believer. In John 6:38-40, Jesus says in verses 38 and 40, *"For I came down from heaven, not to do mine own will, but the will of him that sent me. And this is the will of Him that sent me, that every one which seeth the Son, and believeth on Him, may have everlasting life: and I will raise him up at the last day."* God's will is for everyone who hears about Jesus in any way to establish a relationship with the truth of His Word so that they might have abundant life now and eternal life after death.

Jesus sent the Holy Spirit not only to be a Teacher, but the Holy Spirit is also identified as a Reminder. This second aspect of the Holy Spirit's ministry in us is necessary so that the believer can be reminded of who Jesus is, what He did, and what He will do through the love of the Father. Jesus told the disciples that the Holy Spirit would remind them of whatever He had said to them.

Jesus' Joy is relationship; He gave Himself by the will of the Father so that we might have a loving relationship with Him. The Key to Joy Lies in the Joy of Others means that once we have Jesus' Joy, the relationship that only He can provide and that was purchased for us through His death, burial and resurrection, our joy is fulfilled. Once our joy is fulfilled and because it is maintained by the indwelling presence of the Holy Spirit, we are compelled to share the joy and see to it that the joy is found in others.

The Key to Joy Lies in the Joy of Others!

PART TWO

Pocket Pearls As Tools

Pocket Pearls as Tools

My father's hands were not very big, although he was a big guy. While his hands were not big, I have seen him cut down trees, lift very large objects, and turn a large dining room table upside down. As strong as his hands were, they were also gentle as soft cotton against a baby's face.

Because of his stature and strength, my father was nicknamed "Big O." He grew up on a farm in South Carolina. Not only was my father strong but he was also very handy with a fierce "green thumb" (he could make anything grow). In my adult life, and before marriage, I depended on his ability to find solutions for the things that needed to be fixed in my apartment and to rescue all of my dying plants. After my husband's passing, he was also my "go to guy" for repairs, security scares and flooded basements. It didn't seem to matter what the crisis, I could call my father and he would come to my rescue with the right spirit and the right tools. I am a daddy's girl.

Despite many years of watching my father fix and repair things, I never developed "fix it" skills. I am not a handy person around the house, nor am I acquainted with or have an affinity for tools and gadgets. The digital age also has found me lacking on several fronts. At the writing of this book, I still use a flip phone and am still of the opinion that a cell phone is for emergencies only. However, I am very much aware that the right tools make all the difference in finding solutions for life situations and problems.

The following Pearls are considered "tools" that work in the situations of life that we cannot naturally fix, and for which there is no readily available answer. They are not exhaustive in content; rather, they are a sampling of the many ways the Word of God provides the answers we need. Just as it is essential to have the right tool for repairing and maintaining the many moving parts of life in today's society, it is even more important and essential to have the right spiritual tools to successfully and effectively handle the issues of life. These Pearls represent four tools. The first tool is **service**. It is a tool that can be used to honor and encourage others. The second tool is **forgiveness**. This is a tool that can be used to repair broken and difficult relationships. **Honesty** is the third tool. This tool can be used to let others see the similarities that bring us together as human beings and as vessels needing God's love. Finally, **sharing** is a tool that can be used to connect our lives with each other and to strengthen the ties that bind us together.

Chapter Seven

Pearl Six:
The Seat of Honor is Found at the Seat of Service!

So after he had washed their feet, and had taken his garments, and was set down again, he said unto them, Know ye what I have done to you? Ye call me Master and Lord: and ye say well; for so I am. If I then, your Lord and Master, have washed your feet; ye also ought to wash one another's feet. For I have given you an example, that ye should do as I have done to you (John 13:12-15).

It is amazing to me the importance of where someone sits. Growing up, I remember how we were seated at the dining room table. We grew up having meals together as a family. Before dinner, we were responsible for preparing the necessary plates and utensils and setting the table. My father was always at the head of the table - that was his seat. My mother usually sat next to him and, as the oldest, I was on the other side of him. Our seats reflected our positions in the family and the extent to which those positions were to be regarded. As much as I tried to make certain that my siblings understood and regarded my authority as the oldest, as I remember that time in my life, I recall that my position, while seemingly important, was really that of servant. I had a lot of responsibilities that involved doing things to ensure that my siblings were protected and accounted for. In doing this, I also served my parents as they trusted me to get it done and maintain order while they were away. As is probably the case in many families, my siblings did respond to my leadership but with kicking and screaming and some serious name calling. I could not wait to go off to college where I would no longer have to "serve and protect." I cannot say that my seat at the table and what it represented brought any honor to me.

The Seat of Honor is Found at the Seat of Service is a Pearl of humility. To serve means to wait upon or to care for someone's needs. It suggests placing oneself in a position of providing what is necessary so that the one being served finds and experiences comfort, support or relief. Service is a word that is essential to every aspect of our lives. There are very few, if any, areas of life where service is not anticipated, expected, provided or evaluated. We live in a world where service is necessary and essential to everyday living.

Honor is a word that is often heard when considering the dedication and commitment of the men and women who serve the United States through military service. Their willingness to give their lives defending and protecting the country is acknowledged in many ways. There are holidays and memorials established to commemorate their service. There are also laws and regulations that promote their well being. The idea is that because they have given their lives to keep each citizen out of harm's way and to maintain their freedom, we honor them. In essence, service perpetuates honor.

In John 12, Jesus spoke to a group of people who were curious about following Him. They had heard about His triumphal entry into Jerusalem before the Passover. They also heard that Jesus had raised Lazarus from the dead. In verse 26, Jesus gave them an answer to their curiosity by telling them that following Him meant serving Him. As servants, they would have to practice the same principles of life that He followed. In doing so, they would receive honor from the Father. This honor means to fix valuation upon. Receiving honor from the Father means receiving all of the spiritual benefits that come from life in Christ Jesus. Those benefits are reflected in the two aspects of life Jesus promised — abundant life while we are alive and eternal life when we die.

In the scripture reference for this Pearl (John 13:12-15), Jesus demonstrates how the seat of honor is found at the seat of service. He gives the disciples the greatest lesson on how He loves them. He also shows them how love is demonstrated through serving others. Here, the disciples have been invited to the Passover meal, which was a part of the Passover and the Feast of Unleavened Bread; the most important of the three great annual festivals of Israel. After the meal, Jesus washed the disciples' feet. According to Fred H. Wight, during biblical times, when a guest entered one's home, several acts of kindness and hospitality were shown.[7] Hospitality was considered a sacred duty with specific actions included to express the host's gratitude to God for sending guests to the home. Because guests were believed to be sent by God, the host first bowed, which symbolized the heart, the voice, and the mind were all at the service of the guest. Then an official greeting was given, which might have been followed by a kiss. The shoes of the guests were then removed and guests were offered water for washing of the feet. During the Passover meal, the disciples were not given water to wash their feet; Jesus provided the water, the garment for the washing, and the hands of service to complete the task.

The Bible says in Luke 22:15 that Jesus told the disciples He wanted to eat the Passover meal with them before He suffered. Certainly, the disciples had some idea as to how the evening would progress. They were familiar with and had participated in a Passover meal before. Perhaps what they did not know was that Jesus, the Host for the meal, was going to teach them a lesson in how to serve and receive honor. At the same time, they would see how serving honors those who are served. He served them knowing that He was about to be crucified. He would receive honor from the Father through the resurrection.

Prior to the discourse during the Passover meal, Jesus said, *"If any man serve me, let him follow me; and where I am, there shall also my servant be: if any man serve me, him will my Father honor"* (John 12:26). Jesus' actions during the Passover meal and His words to the disciples before the meal presented an unusual perspective for His followers then, as it also presents the same intriguing perspective to us as Christians today. He was telling the disciples and showing them that, for the Christian, to serve is to honor and to honor is to serve. He said, *"If I then, your Lord and Master, have washed your feet; ye also ought to wash one another's feet"* (John 13:14). That night at the Passover meal, He wanted them to know the love of God through service. He was their Lord and yet, He served them. Jesus served them all the way to the cross. He knew that He was going to die but He also knew that He would be resurrected. The Father would honor His sacrificial service by raising Him from the dead and saving our souls from Hell.

The reality of what Jesus was doing was so foreign to the disciples that, at first, Peter rejected it, thinking that he was not worthy of such love. As mentioned earlier, this is an aspect of the love of God that is still foreign to many. The idea that one must serve in order to demonstrate love and to realize the blessedness of sharing love through service is often difficult to grasp.

Three things that Jesus did during the Passover meal speak to the significance of this Pearl. First, in John 13:12, Jesus asks the disciples a question. He said, *"Know ye what I have done to you?"* He does not give the disciples an opportunity to answer but continues on to answer the question in verses 13 through 15. The interesting thing about the question is that the disciples had been given instructions and directions for preparing for the meal so they were familiar with the experience. In essence, they knew what to do to prepare for the meal, they knew how to prepare for the meal, they knew what to expect during the meal, and they were versed in Jewish custom as it relates to the Passover.

Certainly, they were confident of what would happen and how it would happen.

It appears that Jesus asked the question to begin the process of changing their old way of thinking and to present a new way of thinking. This is evident in what Jesus said after He had washed their feet. In John 13: 34, He said, *"A new commandment I give unto you, That ye love one another; as I have loved you, that ye also love one another."*

It was essential that the disciples understood the significance of Jesus' invitation, preparation, and presentation of the meal. He extended the invitation as the Host for the meal. He prepared the place and the provision because He was the Giver of all things necessary for the meal. He presented the meal in the way that He did because He was about to become the Sacrificial Lamb dying for the sins of the whole world. Jesus' question was a precursor to an example that the disciples needed so that they could clearly see Him as Host, Servant, and Saviour. His question seemed to be designed to cause them to think about what He had just done and to prepare them for what they would have to do. He was preparing them to see honor in the position of servant.

During the Passover meal in Matthew 26:14-24, the disciples bickered among themselves concerning who would be greatest among them. They understood the time Jesus spent with them to be a time of change, yet, in their minds, the change was presented as an opportunity for them to be promoted in their leadership and visibility as followers and trailblazers for a new way of religious thinking. They were like many in today's society who seek honor through various means. The concept of leadership has been taught, packaged and driven into every aspect of modern society. So much so that there are those who equate levels of leadership with levels of honor. The disciples might have equated greatness with honor and were eager to learn "next steps" in the process of being honored. When Jesus asked the disciples if they knew what He had done to them by washing their feet, it may have caused them to think again about their assumptions and predictions about who would be the greatest. They were about to have their way of thinking concerning traditions of greatness challenged and changed.

The second thing Jesus did during the Passover meal that helps us to understand this Pearl is found in verse 13. Jesus says, *"Ye call me Master and Lord: and ye say well; for so I am."* Here, Jesus acknowledges who He is as Master and Lord. He says "*I am,*" which is reminiscent of God's statement to Moses in Exodus chapter three when he was tasked with leading the Nation of Israel out of Egypt. He asked the Lord His name so that he could tell the Nation of Israel who sent him. The Lord replied with the statement, "I AM THAT I AM." Biblical scholars have written volumes to define and describe these words from the Lord. They suggest that these words reflect "the timelessness of God, who is the very foundation of all existence."[8] Before Jesus answered the question about what He had done specifically, He reminded the disciples of Who it was that stood before them. This was necessary in order to provide an unquestionable and indelible understanding of what was taking place that evening. His position and authority during the supper was clear. I believe He reminded them of it to both refocus their attention and prepare their attitudes for what He was about to say.

In the first part of John 13:14, Jesus presents the magnitude of what He did by washing their feet. He did so being Saviour and Servant. In the second part of the verse Jesus tells the disciples that, given what He has just done, they should wash each other's feet. You can imagine what they must have thought upon hearing Jesus' admonishment. Certainly, Peter, who had understood Jesus' actions as an indication of closeness and recognition, had to pause and think about what Jesus was telling them to do. It was one thing to have Jesus, the Saviour of the world to wash his feet, but what could washing his comrade's feet possibly mean for that night. Customarily, when foot washing was done at a special time like this, people were given the elements necessary for foot washing; however, they washed their own feet. As this might have been Peter's thinking, it is possible that each of the disciples had to ponder, consider, and try to decipher Jesus' intent in giving such a direction. Jesus emphasized His position of authority to help the disciples focus on Who He was so that they could understand and appreciate the Saviour as a Servant.

Jesus admonished the disciples to wash each other's feet to help them see that as this was the last time that He would be able to serve them in this way, they must continue to show His love by serving one another. They would honor Him by serving one another.

The third thing that Jesus did during the Passover meal with the disciples is found in verse 15. In this verse, Jesus specifically answers His question to the disciples and gives us the foundation for this Pearl. He told the disciples, *"For I have given you an example, that ye should do as I have done to you."* The Son of God and the Saviour of the world planned and prepared the Passover meal for His friends. The Bible says in Luke 22:15 that Jesus told the disciples He wanted to eat the Passover meal with them before He suffered. He wanted to honor them by serving them.

Prior to the discourse during the Passover meal, Jesus said, *"If any man serve me, let him follow me; and where I am, there shall also my servant be: if any man serve me, him will my Father honor"* (John 12:26). From the Greek, the word honor in this scripture means to fix valuation upon. This is a humbling thought; Jesus honored the disciples through serving them. He told them in Matthew 20:28 that He did not come to be ministered to; rather, He came to minister and to pour out His life for all who would receive of this service. Because He came to serve, the value of His life and death is immeasurable. As He had so faithfully served those whom the Father sent Him to serve, the value of His life and death were carefully and meticulously being presented by the Father to those who followed Him then and those of us who choose to follow Him now. The seat of honor is found at the seat of service — the value of our lives is found in the extent to which we serve according to the Word and will of God.

As Christians, when we serve, it is not the act that is the service, it is the attitude behind the act that reflects service rendered. It is an attitude of love. Jesus manifested love as He served the disciples during the Last Supper. He did what the Apostle Paul describes in Philippians 2:7-8. Jesus, "*...made Himself of no reputation, and took upon Him the form of a servant, and was made in the likeness of men: And being found in fashion as a man, He humbled Himself, and became obedient unto death, even the death of the cross.*" These verses describe and explain how and why Jesus came into this world.

As He served the disciples that night, Jesus made Himself of no reputation, took upon Himself the form or attitude and actions of a servant, and was obedient to the will of God. In Philippians 2:9, the Bible says that because Jesus humbled Himself in this way, God exalted

Him. In loving and then serving the disciples, Jesus honored them and received honor from the Father. Whatever we do in serving, Jesus has given us the example and a commandment to do so.

Jesus demonstrated that the seat of honor is found in the seat of service when He got up from His position at the table. When He got up, He left what was perhaps a comfortable seat. He certainly left a seat of recognized authority. If we desire to follow Jesus' example of love and service, it is essential that we get up from and out of the seat of comfort. Many Christians occupy this seat. It is a seat that has been created through tradition and routine ascribed to the work of the church. We engage in works that allow us to do something, join something, and be the leader over something. In this, it is easier and therefore comfortable to sign up, show up, and busy ourselves with the many things that need to be done in the church. Our works become the focus of serving, while we fail to develop the attitude of a true servant — one who follows the example of Jesus Christ where love is the motivation and position and ease of performance are not considered. When we focus on positions and performance, we often miss opportunities to serve as Jesus did. He served the disciples by getting out of a seat of comfort and into a position of humility.

After getting up from the table that night, the Bible says that Jesus laid aside His garments. This was an outer garment. This piece of clothing was like a jacket or covering that had been exposed to the elements. Serving could not have been done with too many layers. Taking off His outer garment afforded Jesus the ability to shed the weight of the day's activity so that He could move easily and freely. It should be the same with us when we serve. If we, through love, serve one another, we must peel off layers of busyness, biases, cultural differences, stereotypes and all other actions and attitudes that represent the distraction and pull of the world's activity.

After taking off His garments, Jesus girded Himself with a towel, which suggests that the instrument for cleansing was both secure and substantial. The towel was attached to Him so that He could serve without concern for misplacement. It was large enough to be wrapped around Him so that He could wash and dry each of the disciple's feet. This aspect of serving suggests that when we serve, we must make sure that the love of God and the truth of His Word are placed securely in our hearts. This will ensure that as we are presented with opportunities to serve, we have more than enough to meet each need.

Jesus washed the disciples' feet that night to give us an example by which to live. Honor is inherent in service. It is not words, plaques, money, fortune or fame. Honor is that which flows from the heart of the servant and returns to the heart as the service is rendered. It is intangible, indisputable and always available to the servant who is willing.

It has taken many years for me to put this Pearl in proper perspective in my life. I think for a long time, I was so "busy" serving that I could not grasp the importance of having a servant's attitude such as Jesus demonstrated. I also could not see how honor comes with serving. This is what is essential in how we serve as Christians. Doing is not serving and serving is not doing. In the scripture reference for this Pearl (John 13:12), Jesus asked the disciples if they understood what He had done to them by washing their feet. I believe He wanted them to understand that washing their feet was not just an act. It was not a gesture of recognition presented to acknowledge the efforts of the team. Nor was it a deed of commendation given as a reward for faithful service. Perhaps His question was designed to draw from them a greater focus on the love that compelled the act and the real benefit of the act. When we through love serve one another, we honor them. As we honor them, we honor the Lord. When we honor the Lord, He honors us with the grace that is necessary to serve again and again and again.

The Seat of Honor is Found at the Seat of Service!

Chapter Eight

Pearl Seven:
Bake Your Bread in the Ovens of Others!

And be ye kind one to another, tender-hearted, forgiving one another, even as God for Christ's sake hath forgiven you (Ephesians 4:32).

Certainly, the words in this Pearl need interpreting. When I first heard these words from my husband, I did not understand them at all. He never really fully explained to me what this Pearl meant and it has taken some time for me to fully understand this statement. I realize that at the time my husband shared this statement with me, he knew that I did not understand it and that I was not ready to live according to the Pearl or effectively use it as a tool for my life.

My husband was my best friend, and like most women, I shared all of my cares, concerns, stories, struggles, problems, secrets, challenges, insecurities and all other "me" stuff with him. I probably required more of his attention than he had brain space to give; however, I know that he was listening to me. This is an aspect of who he was that blessed me beyond words. I believe that there is an art and a science to listening. There are books, theories and principles regarding this essential ability. Thankfully, my husband was blessed with an unusual and seemingly divine ability to listen — to be present for the words and feelings of others.

My husband and I worked together in ministry for nine years. In the early years of working together, I struggled with the idea of working in the church — I wanted to go off and get a doctorate so that I could become the president of a college. My husband was truly a steadying force for me. His gentle yet persuasive guidance helped me learn and grow in understanding that ministry consistently required our attention and that my need for attention and my desire to pursue a "great career" had to more often than not take a back seat to preaching the Gospel. You can imagine how I responded when I was given this husbandly insight. Thank God for grace and growth.

Because we were both in full-time ministry, we were constantly engaged in activities that involved caring for and assisting with the concerns of others. Admittedly, I had many insecurities and my need for my husband's attention did not make the requirement for selflessness in caring for others an easy task. I often found myself unloading concerns for what I thought was mistreatment by others. At first, I didn't get it but every time I shared what I considered a hurt or offense from one of the members of the church or even a family member, my husband had the same response - "they didn't mean it like that." I usually tried to assure him that the offense was committed on purpose and I was sure that they "did mean it." I just could not understand how he was not moved or offended by what I thought were hurtful words and rude actions of others. I was not as "tenderhearted" as he was. I did not know how to forgive *before* the offense could even become a source of irritation that would reach my mouth and turn into words that did not edify. The offense would then taint my heart so that my thoughts were not pure, lovely, honest, just, and of a good report (Philippians 4:8). It was not until after his passing that I realized that I did not know how to *bake my bread in the ovens of others.*

The scripture reference for this Pearl is Ephesians 4:32. In this verse, the word "kind" comes from a Greek word that means *to furnish what is needed.* In this epistle, the Apostle

Paul is instructing believers at the Church at Ephesus in practical Christian duties. Verse 32 admonishes the believer to be kind; to furnish what is necessary - a tender heart that is ready to forgive. This is the kind of heart that pleases God and allows for maximum growth and development amongst believers. Forgiveness is, in my estimation, the most freeing aspect of life.

It used to be that when I was hurt or offended because of what I thought was a lack of kindness or concern from others, I shielded myself by saying, "it doesn't matter because God loves me." I have come to realize that it (what **they** did) does not matter; however, **they do** matter because God loves them as He loves me. Therefore, I must always be the first to forgive because the Bread of Life (Jesus) has been so wonderfully prepared in my heart. He was and is the Source of true forgiveness. I must give what is necessary — forgiveness, in order that the heart of the one I have forgiven may be the oven in which the Bread of Life may also be warmed. Baking one's bread in the oven of another means forgiving first, before the offense has opportunity to "rise" and become the bitter bread of unkind words and hurtful actions. When this happens, it is virtually impossible to forgive according to the Word of God.

I had an opportunity to pray during a prayer breakfast for Still I Rise, a non-profit organization for men and women who have suffered domestic violence. Rear Admiral Barry C. Black, the 62nd Chaplain of the United States Senate, who was the guest speaker for the event, described the last four verses in Ephesians 4 as the "Conspiracy of Kindness." He suggests that kindness must be strategically and intentionally developed in the life of the believer. Chaplain Black says that there are four requirements for the conspiracy. First, one must see verbal abuse as a danger signal; it is the prelude to physical abuse. Second, one must seek to always build others up. Third, one must practice the presence of God. Lastly, one must learn to forgive. In his exhortation, he expounded on the significance of forgiveness as an aspect of kindness and as an essential tool in moving forward past challenges. Forgiveness is where the Bread of Life is allowed to rise and fill the nostrils of the soul and spirit with a sweet savor.

According to the History Channel, in all its various forms, bread is the most widely consumed food in the world. Bread has been a staple and a significant source of nourishment for mankind for thousands of years.[9] It has been declared a healthy and nutritious food that fills the stomach as well as the soul. Bread has many forms, is found in every culture, and is still enjoyed daily in most ancient simplicity. All over the world, people are acquainted with and consider bread as an essential food source. Whether white, wheat, whole grain, with or without gluten, low calorie, hot dog bun, honey bun, bagel, donut, croissant, biscuit, biscotti or vanilla wafer, regardless of how it is or was prepared, sliced, baked, or produced, this simple yet universally accepted food item has been, in some way, an integral part of our diet.

This is perhaps a part of the significance of Jesus' description of Himself as the Bread of Life. In John 6:35, in response to a question concerning His authenticity as the Son of God, Jesus told a group of followers, "*...I am the bread of life: he that cometh to me shall never hunger; and he that believeth on me shall never thirst.*" In this instance, Jesus appealed to the mind and understanding of the Jewish listeners who might have thought about the Tabernacle of Moses, which was a sacred place where God met His people, the Israelites. It was the place where the Priests and the people came together for worship and to offer sacrifices. They did this because, during that time, there was no perfect and complete sacrifice that could allow a living relationship between God and man. In the Tabernacle, there was a place that was known as the Holy Place where there was an altar that had bread called the "Bread of the Presence," which comprised 12 cakes placed on the table of showbread.[10] It was referred to as the Bread of Presence because it was always in the Holy Place, having been placed there by the Priest. The Holy Place in the

Tabernacle was the dwelling place of the Lord; therefore, this bread was to be always in the Lord's presence. The bread was representative of "manna," the bread that the Lord gave from Heaven to the Nation of Israel when they were in the wilderness.

As the Bread of Presence was a reminder of God's provision to His people, it served two purposes: it indicated that God was willing to fellowship with man and it represented the nourishment that God and only God had given them. In John 6:35-47, Jesus paints a very vivid and complete picture of His presence as the Bread of Life. He tells His followers that as God provided bread from Heaven for the Nation of Israel to sustain them in their journey in the wilderness, He provided Jesus as the Bread of Life to sustain the believer in a sin-sick world. He came from Heaven as the only permanent satisfaction for the human desires of life and He is the mainstay that satisfies every man's hunger for real life.

In order to forgive, there must be a Source of sustaining power that affords the forgiver the ability to truly forgive. The sustaining power can only come from the Giver of life and the symbol of all forgiveness — Jesus, the Bread of Life. Forgiveness is the path by which my bread (my born-again, Holy Spirit-filled spirit man) has opportunity to be effective and impactful in the life of another. By forgiving, I begin a process of spiritual exchange that renders my spirit vulnerable or open to the Holy Spirit so that the Word of God is given to and prayerfully received by the one to whom the forgiveness is given.

In order to bake my bread in the ovens of others, the baking process begins with my forgiveness. I can and must forgive because I am forgiven. The process is like baking natural bread. It initially goes into the oven and is, at first, just a lump of dough; there is some form but what it will be is not evident to the senses. When I choose to forgive, there is an internal releasing of all and any need to defend self or get even with the one for whom forgiveness is being given.

I can remember my mother's biscuits baking. We watched as she put flour, a pinch of salt, and a good amount of lard together in a bowl (even saying the word lard in this day and time seems taboo - but it was good). I am not sure of what other ingredients might have been included, but I remember these with certainty. She worked with the ingredients until they were just stiff enough to pat and form into perfect biscuits. I know that some people use a biscuit cutter to shape them, but my mother used her hands (I think that made for extra love in the biscuit). After forming them, she greased an old beat up, round metal pan and placed each biscuit in it. The table had flour on it, her hands were messy with flour and lard, the oven was hot, and stomachs were ready. But, the process was just beginning. We had to wait for those biscuits to heat up, rise and then turn golden brown before we could eat them. Like baking natural bread, the process of forgiveness begins with a simple knowing, based on the Word of God, that it is necessary. To this knowing, an attitude of humility that says "because I have been forgiven, I must forgive" must be added. Once these two ingredients come together, forgiveness is then shaped, patted and molded by the power of the Holy Spirit in the forgiver's heart until it is ready to be placed in the oven, that is the heart of the one needing forgiveness.

As my mother's biscuits were baking, the smell of those warm and delectable pieces of bread made us anxious to have one in our little hands. The smell was so appealing that we started preparing for them to come out of the oven well before they were done. We would get the knife, the butter, and some jelly, honey or syrup (whichever happened to be available at the time) to crown them with just the right accompaniments for a delicious and satisfying treat. When my mother's biscuits came out of the oven, there was no wondering as to what we were going to do with them. They were not going to stay in the pan long, they would not get cold, and the possibility of having more than one was out of the question. This meant that once we got our hands on one of those biscuits, we had to savor it, take our time with it, and enjoy every moment of Mama's biscuits. They were a treat - almost like dessert. She did not make them often and when she did, we knew that love and a desire to nourish our bodies in a special way were the unseen ingredients. As a result, if she could have received money for every ooh, ah, and "these are the best biscuits in the world," she would have been a very wealthy woman.

Like the natural process of baking, once the truth of God's Word and humility have been shaped and formed by the power of the Holy Spirit, it is ready to be warmed in the heart of the one who is forgiven. Like my mother's biscuits, forgiveness must be placed in the recipient's heart if it is to become more than a thought or a knowing of what is right to do. I must bake my bread, that is, deposit the truth with love and out of a humble heart, into the life of those for whom forgiveness is needed. When I do so, I must do so with a confidence that as the Holy Spirit has formed and shaped my forgiveness for the exact purpose for which it is needed, I do not have to concern myself with what will happen to it or how it will be received. When I have truly allowed my bread to be baked in the oven of another, I will sense the aroma of a simple lump of humility clothed in the Word of God being warmed into greater and deeper relationship with God and man. In many instances, we may never know the extent to which the bread we have baked in the ovens of others has been prepared and served to satisfy a hungry soul. Our duty and responsibility is only to prepare the ingredients, the truth of God's Word and humility of heart, and allow the Holy Spirit to mold and shape it for placement in the heart of another.

Bake your Bread in the Ovens of Others is a Pearl of forgiveness. Jesus is the Bread of Life. He is that nourishment without which we cannot live nor have life. Once we have life in Christ, we are empowered by the Holy Spirit to forgive. No matter how difficult it may have been for you to forgive, and no matter how horrible or unforgiveable the offense may have been, God desires that we do what our Saviour did - forgive. Bake your bread in the oven of another. The aroma of forgiveness is beyond description and has benefits beyond our understanding.

Bake Your Bread in the Ovens of Others!

Chapter Nine

Pearl Eight:
The Most Honorable Trait is The Character of Honesty! The Ultimate in Growth is Transparency! The Ultimate in Self Respect is Self-Appreciation!

Be of the same mind one toward another. Mind not high things, but condescend to men of low estate. Be not wise in your own conceits. Recompense to no man evil for evil. Provide things honest in the sight of all men (Romans 12:16-17).

As much as I remember being a very good little girl and very obedient, I will never forget my childhood lies. I wanted so badly to be viewed as "good" that any time I encountered a situation that might have shed a negative light on my otherwise good little girl character, I would say what was necessary to get through the situation. Even the best taught Sunday school lesson heralding the dangers of telling a tale did not sink into my mind well enough to cause me not to hide behind a lie. Trying to please others and promote self by saying what you think is best, but is not the truth, is lying. I lied because I wanted my parents to think well of me, always. I was an "A" student, I was not involved in my peers' bad behaviors, and I worked hard at being the perfect "big sister."

While childhood folly may seem small and insignificant, unaddressed childhood lies are often the seed of dishonesty in our adult lives. I had to grow to learn that being seemingly perfect is not what causes others to notice you, care about you or love you. I needed to learn that honesty and transparency are essential to one's character. Ironically, even when I became a Christian, I had difficulty overcoming the tendency to lie to please others and be accepted. Spiritually, I needed to grow up and learn that honesty and transparency are essential to one's character. A life lived without honesty and transparency is a misrepresentation of who we are. It suggests that we do not respect and appreciate who and how God made us. Years of pursuit of a real relationship with Him and His graciousness in allowing me to marry a man whose character was bathed in transparency have helped me to strive to live a transparent life. Please note the word "strive"; living an honest and transparent life requires a constant process of self-examination and spiritual purging. I still struggle at times with seeing myself as God sees me and accepting who He made me to be. When I struggle in this area, it is easy for me to project that I am "fine" when, honestly, I am hurting and the image that others see is not really what exists. With this Pearl, I can honestly say that I have not arrived but I am glad that the Pearl and the scriptures that support it are a constant source of encouragement and direction for growth.

The scripture reference to this Pearl is from the Apostle Paul's letter to the church at Rome. In chapter 12, Paul provides practical steps that members of the church should follow in order to live a good Christian life. His admonishment in verse 17 is simple — Christians should avoid getting even when wronged and they should live honestly. Paul admonished the church to "provide" things honest. The word provide in this context means to take thought in advance or to think about beforehand. The phrase "things honest" is a rendering of a single Greek word that means, that which is fitting and useful. In essence, Paul was telling the church to take thought in advance so that they would present what is fitting and useful to others. To live honestly in this context means to think about, care about and determine to live in a way that one's manner of life or lifestyle reflects what is on the inside. In 2 Corinthians 8:21, Paul uses the same words (provide for honest things) in describing the method of handling the affairs of the church. He thought carefully beforehand and performed his duties openly in the sight of God and man. This aspect of his ministry and character was essential to eliminating suspicion among his peers and those who followed his ministry.

Living an honest and transparent life is essential. Christians must take thought beforehand and think about what we present to the world as our life and lifestyle so that **what we say** and **what we do** are a true indication of **Who we say** is on the inside. We do this so that there is no suspicion or criticism of the Gospel. Our honesty and transparency are necessary so that the world will know that our God is God and that Jesus Christ is Lord.

There is nothing hidden from the Lord and yet we often present our lives to others with a façade that is meant to give a specific impression of who we are. What we say and what we do may appear to reflect the integrity of a life hidden in Christ. However, a close examination (in times when adversity and the trials of life beat against the façade that we have so carefully built) often reveals a weak, and in many instances, underdeveloped spirit. There is no evidence of the power of God through the work of the Holy Spirit.

Examining our lives to make certain that honesty and transparency are present is like the process of finding a good apple. It takes time and attention, but once found, a good apple is the source of great delight and eating pleasure. I love apples and until recently they were the central component of my breakfast each day. All apples basically have the same characteristics as it relates to nutrient content. They contain antioxidants, which are disease-fighting compounds; they contain fiber, which has a host of health benefits; and they contain vitamins and minerals, which help to make the body functional. Because they come in different shapes and sizes, the amount of nutrients and calories may vary; however, apples consumed as a part of the American diet all have beneficial features. While they have the same beneficial features, I am partial to the taste and texture of the Fuji apple. I have tried several different types of apples but the Fuji reigns supreme in my book.

When you love apples, what is most distressing and of complete frustration is going through the process of examining, choosing, and then purchasing what looks like a good apple and cutting into it to find that what it appears to be on the outside is not what is on the inside. Finding rot, worms or even mush (apple pulp that is beginning to decay) is both disappointing and discouraging. This is what happens when we live our lives without honesty and transparency. When people see us, they expect that what we look like on the outside is a reflection of what is on the inside. They approach us based on that reflection. When they approach, what they should get when they engage in conversation and association with us is the truth of God's Word. Even if they never have a conversation with us, the lifestyle we live should so effectively reflect the love of God and the character of Christ that they can receive what is on the inside by our example. The inside of who we are should reflect in our communication and conduct — this is done through honesty and transparency. Self examination that reveals and then removes anything that does not allow our lives to reflect the truth of God's Word is necessary in order to live an honest and transparent life.

Honesty and transparency are necessary in order for us to better reflect – externally and internally – our Lord and Saviour so that others may "taste and see that He is good." As this Pearl states, in order to grow as a Christian, transparency is necessary. We must present things honest in the sight of God and man. Transparency is first necessary before God because He knows us and is acquainted with all of our ways. He is our Creator and Maker; there is nothing about any aspect of our lives that He does not know — including the things we may be trying to cover up from others. The Bible says that there is nothing that is hidden from Him (Psalm 139:1-3). He is especially desirous of revealing, exposing and ultimately removing anything that does not resemble His nature, which is love.

According to Hebrews 12:5-11, because God loves us (with a love that cannot be comprehended with the natural mind), He corrects us when there is something on the inside that is not right according to His Word. Our Father to child relationship with Him is evident in that correction. This correction is essential to growth and development as a Christian.

Hebrews 12:5 and Proverbs 3:11 both contend that we should not despise or loathe chastening from the Lord. The word chastening or chastisement means training through correction, including instruction that leads to discipline. When the Lord chastises us, His love is evident in that training is taking place and instruction is provided with the chastisement. What should ultimately happen is that the correction will lead to discipline, as we are obedient to chastisement's inherent training and instruction.

While chastisement in the form of correction is not necessarily what we want to receive, it is God's way of helping us to conform to His image. God desires to show us and help us to change whatever is on the inside that can hinder or threaten our relationship with Him and our ability to be an example of His love. Because God loves us, we are cared for and nurtured in a manner that requires our Father to do what is necessary that we might grow up to be "just like Him."

His correction is an aspect of His love and it is given to us to discipline us so that nothing hinders our growth. When we grow, God is glorified (John 15:8) and the world, our brothers and sisters in Christ, our families and anyone in our sphere of influence can see that the God we serve is real and that Jesus Christ is Lord.

Honesty and transparency are perhaps difficult for us as Christians because, like most aspects of our Christian walk, they are very much related to how we feel about others and ourselves. It is just not easy to expose our feelings but in order to live in honesty and transparency, we must move beyond our feelings and live in the truth of God's Word.

I believe that Hebrews 12:1-2 provides the first step in the process of moving beyond what we feel. It says that we must, "*...lay aside every weight, and the sin which doth so easily beset us, and let us run with patience the race that is set before us, Looking unto Jesus the Author and Finisher of our faith; who for the joy that was set before Him endured the cross, despising the shame, and is set down at the right hand of the throne of God.*" In order to move beyond our feelings, we must put down the weight of natural impulses and worldly viewpoints, acknowledge the sin that results when we focus on those feelings, and **run with**

patience; that is, continue to do what we know is the truth with patience.

Jesus is our example of what it means to move past feelings to do the will of the Father. As He was 100 percent human and 100 percent divine, certainly His humanity caused different feelings that ran counter to what was necessary for Him to go to the cross. The Bible provides us with many examples of His human feelings and His response to those feelings. He wept and felt sorrow, He felt hunger and looked for food, He felt compassion and healed the sick, and He felt concern and made provision for His mother.

Perhaps the most vivid yet magnificent example of Jesus' ability to move past His feelings is found in the Bible's account of His time in the Garden at Gethsemane. After the Last Supper on the night before He was to be crucified, Jesus took the disciples to the Garden of Gethsemane to pray. With a full knowledge of the kind of death He would soon face, one can only imagine the magnitude of Jesus' feelings and emotions. In the Garden, Mark 14:33 tells us that He began to be "*sore amazed and very heavy.*" This verse in the Amplified version of the Bible says He "*began to be struck with terror and amazement and deeply troubled and depressed.*"

While verse 33 records His sentiments, Mark 14:34 gives the words He used to describe how He was feeling. He said, *"My soul is exceeding sorrowful unto death..."* The Amplified Version of the verse says, "*My soul is exceedingly sad (overwhelmed with grief) so that it almost kills Me!...*" Jesus experienced an emotional and mental pressure that no one can ever know.

When He said that His soul was exceeding sorrowful, it suggested that His feelings and emotions were challenged with grief and distress that were beyond human ability to understand and accept.

The weight of the responsibility of the cross was so great that Jesus prayed to the Lord that He might escape the horror of the crucifixion. He said in Luke 22:42, "*Father, if thou be willing, remove this cup from me...*" In Mark 14:36a Jesus said, "*Abba Father, all things are possible unto thee; take away this cup from me.*" His feelings and emotions were so strong that He sought to gain relief from the suffering that would surely be experienced on the cross. In these words, He exposed His feelings to the Father in prayer. He was honest and transparent.

There are times in our lives when the pressure of life presents catastrophic situations that were unexpected and certainly unwelcomed. There are also times when we have to make choices that all seem to have unwanted and uncertain consequences. In these times, the easiest thing to do is to just walk away from the situation and refuse to choose. However, these times call for honesty and transparency with ourselves and with God. This is what Jesus did in the Garden and it is the example that helps us as Christians to press beyond the difficulties and the challenges of life. As was the case with Jesus, God is ever present to hear our cry and to provide what is needed so that we can have victory over every circumstance. I know, you are probably saying, that was Jesus, this is me. I get it. I too have dealt with difficulties that were seemingly insurmountable and beyond my ability to cope. What we must see and understand about Jesus' example is that the same God who heard Him and strengthened Him is the same God who is present to strengthen you through that challenge and help you through the difficulties of life. Because He is our Father, not only **can** He help us, He **wants** to help us.

As Jesus moved past His feelings and emotions to be honest and transparent in prayer to the Father, He also submitted His will to the will of the Father. When we are honest and transparent and move past our feelings to expose ourselves to the Lord, the next step is submission to His will. In each of the Gospel's account of Jesus in the Garden, He surrenders to the Father's will. In Mark 14:36b Jesus said, *"nevertheless not what I will, but what thou wilt."* These words suggest that even with the weight of the crucifixion, Jesus was aware of His Father's presence and His desire to help Him. Luke 22:43 says that after He sought to escape the suffering of the cross and when He ultimately surrendered to the will of the Father, the Lord sent an angel from Heaven to strengthen Him. How magnificent is this! Jesus' examples of transparency and honesty in the presence of great suffering should encourage us to endeavor to be honest and transparent with the Lord. He knows what you are going through. Not only does He know what you are going through but He knows you. He created you and knows exactly what you need to move past your feelings to receive His help and experience victory that only He can give. I encourage you to take a moment right now to talk to the Lord. Tell Him what you have been feeling that you have not been honest with yourself about. When we are honest with ourselves through transparency with God in prayer, we open the way for Him to minister to us through His Word. This is what He wants to do because He is our Father.

Once we have been transparent and honest with the Father and submit to His will, we are then equipped to be transparent in our dealings with others. The key to presenting things honest in the sight of men is first being changed and strengthened through transparency with the Lord.

The strength we receive from Him allows us to "clean up" our lives so that the life and lifestyle we present to others is honest and open for examination. When this happens, our lives can be used as instruments of God's love and peace. We become living examples of the power of God's Word to change our lives.

I have had my share of catastrophic and earth shattering situations. When I heard the words, "he's gone" when my husband died, the grief, pain, agony and fear that filled my mind caused me to want to stop breathing, stop thinking, stop seeing, stop hearing — I just wanted everything to stop. I could not think beyond the moment and I felt so alone and helpless that all I knew was that everything just needed to stop so that I could get a hold of myself. I really did not want to process what I heard. I did not want to believe what I heard and I certainly did not want to deal with what I heard. My feelings and emotions were beyond control and I lost it. It took a long time to push past my emotions and live normally and pro-ductively after my husband's death. There were many times when I just could not get it together. However, what I have had to do over all these years is to be honest with myself and with the Lord. I have told the Lord that I was angry with Him, that there is no need for me to exist, that I could not preach again, that I must have been a bad wife because Steve chose Heaven over me; the list goes on and on. The tumultuous wave of thoughts and feelings that have filled my mind have been many. I thank God for His tender mercy, patience and loving kindness toward me. He knows me and has kept me so that I am able to say every day - God is faithful (1 Corinthians 10:13).

Like Jesus, I have gotten to the place where I just wanted out and over. Also, like Jesus, I have learned to submit to the will of the Father. Thankfully, each time I have cried out to the Lord He has heard me, comforted me and then ministered to me that He will never leave me or forsake me. He has assured me that no matter what it looks like or feels like, I am victorious because of Christ.

Honesty and transparency are necessary in order for us to grow as Christians. God's love for us is so powerful that He does not allow us to remain in a place where there are things on the inside that will hinder our growth. Accordingly, He corrects us and affords us an opportunity to be restored to continue to grow. We are equipped through the Power of the Holy Spirit to do what Jesus did — to move past our feelings and to be honest and transparent in our Christian lives. The ultimate in growth is transparency and the most honorable trait is the character of honesty.

The Most Honorable Trait is The Character of Honesty!

The Ultimate in Growth is Transparency! The Ultimate in Self Respect is Self-Appreciation!

(These will allow for maximum utility by God)

Chapter Ten

Pearl Nine:
Love Compels One to Share!
Love Accepts Correction and
Welcomes Reproof!

But whoso hath this world's good, and seeth his brother have need, and shutteth up his bowels of compassion from him, how dwelleth the love of God in him? (I John 3:17)

We hardly ever hear the word "share" these days. It seems that it has been replaced with sophisticated concepts like collaboration, merging, and networking. These terms fit the technology-driven approach to being engaged in conversation or communicating with one another. Social media has seemingly replaced the face-to-face exchange that once allowed people to look each other in the eye, revealing the commonality of human frailty in order to share things, thoughts, ideas and even, heartfelt concern.

I grew up in a household with seven children and, for many years, a short, yet feisty grandmother. My parents and my grandmother sang the "share with your brothers and sisters" song so much that, as children, we sang the song to each other when we were unable to get what we wanted from a sibling. As children, McDonald's French-fries were number one on the "no share" list. Unfortunately, the "share with your brothers and sisters song" was often used to pry one or two of those tasty pieces out of the reluctant hand of a sister or brother.

As much as we did not like it, our parents' admonishments to share were preparing us to create a bond as siblings that would afford us close relationships with each other. Learning how to have good relationships as siblings would ultimately lead each of us to a saving knowledge of and relationship with the Lord. It wasn't just French-fries that we shared; we grew up learning to demonstrate care through sharing. Over the past several years, our sharing has led us to stay together as a family, enjoying countless celebrations including a yearly family vacation. What we learned about sharing as children has also kept us together as a family in times of adversity and loss.

To share means to partake of, use, experience, or enjoy with others. It implies a mutual exchange that includes enjoyment. The idea that sharing involves a mutual exchange suggests that both the sharer and the recipient of what is being shared benefit from the exchange. Compassion and relationship are the benefits of sharing.

Love Compels One to Share is a Pearl of compassion. To have and show compassion means to have a sympathetic consciousness of others' distress, together with a desire to alleviate it. Having compassion means having a true sense of the needs of others and being ready, willing, and able to address that need. Compassion is essential to sharing.

The scripture reference for this Pearl is taken from the Apostle John's letter to the Early Church. It was written to instruct and encourage members of the Church who were facing challenges that might have caused them to be weak in faith. In I John 3, John encourages believers to be strong in the faith by having confidence in their salvation and practicing deeds of love. Verse 16 says, *"Hereby perceive we the love of God, because he laid down his life for us: and we ought to lay down our lives for the brethren."* This verse gives the basis for the love that believers should have and demonstrate toward one another. It tells us that God was willing to send Jesus to die for us because He so loved us. Verse 17, the scripture for this Pearl, provides an example of what should be done in response to God's love for us and in light of a brother or a sister's need. Christians were to be motivated by the love of God to allow compassion to be moved to action and share.

In the scripture verse for this Pearl, someone who has this world's good and does not show compassion is someone who has an ample and consistent set of resources. It is someone who also sees that others have need but does not share. Having described such a person, the scripture goes on to ask the question, if one has ample resources and is aware of the needs of others but does not share those resources, how can the love of God reside in him? The question suggests that if the love of God is in us, then there is no way that we can withhold from someone in need what is needed — because of love, we are compelled to share.

God's best is that our sharing is presented and supported through the love we receive from Him. We share and continue to share because His love fills our hearts. This kind of sharing was demonstrated in the Early Church. Acts 4:32-37 describes three aspects of the sharing atmosphere of the Church. First, they were all believers; that is, they believed on the Lord Jesus Christ and confessed that He was Lord. Secondly, they were of one heart and one soul. This means that the believers had the love of God in their hearts and had renewed their minds to follow

Christ's example. Loving God and following the example of Christ meant that they would see the needs of others as an opportunity to share love and their possessions. The third aspect of the atmosphere of sharing was that the believers had all things common. Having all things common meant that they made their resources open and available to all. Once their possessions were available to all, Acts 4:35 says that, *"distribution was made unto every man according as he had need."*

Certainly, the sharing atmosphere of the Early Church differs from that of today's Church setting. While the idea of having all things common is still evident in the charitable contributions that are made in the Church, there are also organizations that exist to provide for those in need. With the number of churches and other organizations that assist or support those in need, knowing what, when and how to share can be difficult to determine. Certainly, identifying what is or is not a need can be subjective and hard to decide. In today's society, we are often confronted with scenarios that describe the plight of persons in need. As an example, there are countless advertisements and commercials depicting people who are homeless, hungry or without help to maintain their lives. These ads are designed to cause those who have ample and consistent resources to share them. Given this modern atmosphere for sharing, how do we share?

I encourage you to focus on the words of the scripture reference for this Pearl and remember that sharing begins with compassion. If you are not certain that you are sharing in a manner that is pleasing to God, ask yourself the following questions:

1. Is the love of God in my heart?
2. Have my basic needs been supplied so that my life is sustained?
3. How can I share the love of God with what I have?

We share out of and because of the love of God in our hearts. What we share — whether material substance, time and service, or words and experiences — depends on how compassion is moved to action based on the level of love in our hearts. It really is between you and God.

Even with the love of God in our hearts, we live in a time where societal norms and a barrage of information create perceptions that may cause us to limit or even withhold sharing. With false advertising, scams, and various schemes designed to lure our possessions away from us under false pretenses, it is easy to have misgivings about sharing one's resources when a need is presented. Given the atmosphere of the world we live in, it is necessary to pray for wisdom and seek guidance from an authority when needs are presented and we desire to share.

Just as our sharing may be hindered by perceptions created by schemes, it is also possible that sharing can be hindered by an improper attitude. Sharing requires the proper attitude. In order to have the proper attitude toward sharing, it is important that our care and compassion are not limited or stifled by being judgmental.

John 7:24 speaks to the manner in which those who love God should approach all situations in life — especially when it is necessary to share. In this chapter, Jesus was at the Feast of Tabernacles where He went into the Temple and taught. Before teaching in the Temple, He had healed a sick man on the Sabbath Day — an action considered against Jewish law. People were amazed at how He taught and the miracles He performed but there were also those who opposed Him and wanted Him silenced. Jesus' healing someone on the Sabbath Day was just one act included in a set of accusations designed to discredit Him. In essence, there was division among the people as to whether or not Jesus was who He claimed to be. In the midst of the argument concerning His identity and authenticity, Jesus said, *"Judge not according to the appearance, but judge righteous judgment."* In essence, Jesus told the people that they should not discern or esteem a situation based on sight alone. While they esteemed Jesus as a breaker of the law, what they missed was the need of the sick man to be healed and, most especially, the love and compassion that Jesus had shown in healing him. Their judgmental attitudes hindered their ability to see the wonderful works of the Saviour.

When we judge others or situations based only on what we see or think we see, it is possible to develop an improper attitude about sharing. When this happens and we withhold from or do not respond to the needs of others, our ability to share can be compromised. Jesus' response to His accusers is the foundation for the proper attitude for sharing. The word righteous in John 7:24 means just or correct. In this context, it also means good, beautiful, and useful. Jesus admonished His accusers not to decide a matter with a superficial glance; rather, they should see beyond the immediate and see through the eyes of compassion what is good, beautiful and useful. God is the only One who can know the heart of man; therefore, He is the only One who can determine motives and intentions. This is why our sharing must be motivated by the love of God. When we are motivated by the love of God, we trust that He will lead and guide us in our sharing. Not only do we trust that He will guide us in our sharing, we also trust that the outcome of our sharing is in His hands. Ultimately, He will judge the intents of every heart.

Love compels one to share is also a Pearl of relationship. Sharing begins with care or compassion (voluntary or forced - in the case of my siblings) and ends with relationship. Because sharing begins with compassion and involves a mutual exchange, it presents an opportunity for establishing, maintaining and continuing loving relationships.

Relationship means to have some quality or aspects that connect two or more things or parts as being, belonging or working together. With sharing, the quality that connects is compassion. When we share out of a heart of love, compassion allows a connection to be established. As you read this you may be thinking, if you chose to share, how can each instance of sharing produce a connection that leads to relationships?

The connection that is established through sharing is intangible yet recognizable. Because we share out of love for God and with the love of God, the connection is spiritual. That is, it is beyond our ability to comprehend with the mind and it is more than valuable than the things we can see, touch, taste, smell or hear. The connection cannot be perceived with the senses, we know and appreciate the connection in the heart. Once we share out of love for God and with the love that God has given us, we promote and demonstrate the oneness that is the core of being in the family of God.

In 1 John 3, after the Apostle John admonished members of the Early Church to share, he explained the connection that results. Verses 18 and 19 read, *"My little children, let us not love in word, neither in tongue; but in deed and in truth. And hereby we know that we are of the truth, and shall assure our hearts before Him.* Verse 18 tells us that we should not attempt to demonstrate love with lip service; rather, as Christians, our love must be shown through action that is not hypocritical but sincere because of the truth of God's Word that is in us. Verse 19 tells us that when our actions are prompted by love, we know that we are a part of the family of God because of the Truth that is in us. Not only is there an assurance of the connection that we have to God and with each other, but sharing with the right attitude allows us to have an "assured heart." One interpretation of this verse says, *"In this way we shall become fully aware that to the truth we owe our lives, and in His presence our hearts shall be at peace."* We can be at peace with God knowing that through His love, we have not withheld our resources from those who are in need.

When I think about what I have shared and what has been shared with me, I am convinced that the greatest thing that I have shared and that has been shared with me is the invitation to become a part of the family of God. While the scripture reference for this Pearl relates to sharing of "this world's goods," one of the greatest resources we have is time. When we take time and use it in actions of witnessing or sharing the Good News of Jesus Christ, the benefits are far beyond what we can imagine.

I will never forget Jean, the woman who took time to share Jesus Christ with me. I have not spoken to her in more than 30 years and yet we are connected because we are a part of the family of God. I am sure that because of the love of God that prompted her to share back then, she is certainly enjoying the blessedness of the peace of God today. She shared Jesus with me while I was working and preparing to attend graduate school. I was a faithful churchgoer and had been baptized, but had not fully committed my life to Christ. Jean had consistently lived an exemplary life before me. She was a humble and quiet woman with an unassuming presence. While she seemed to be nice and we occasionally chatted, I had made a judgment call that she was not a person that I would want to associate with. I thought she did not dress the way progressive professionals should dress. I also thought that she was a bit plain and could use a little makeup (at least lipstick). Additionally, Jean did not attempt to be a part of the many cliques that were common to the building and she never attended any of the office social functions.

One day, we happened to be in a boardroom alone when she changed the topic of our lunchtime conversation and began to share from her heart. She looked into my face, told me that I was looking for something that I would never find until I accepted Jesus – the Giver of life. The quick change in conversation and her sincere gaze into my eyes startled, challenged, and comforted me at the same time. Her words pierced my heart and confirmed what I had been unknowingly dealing with on the inside; I was empty even though I had tried to fill my head with knowledge and my life with success. My heart was empty and I needed to be rescued. I needed a Saviour who could fill my heart and change my way of thinking. We stood in a conference room in the building where I had only been employed for a little over a year. She did not pray with me and did not badger me. She simply spoke to a place on the inside of me that needed to hear what she said but, more importantly, needed to be changed so that I could have real life. Later that week, in the quietness of my little apartment alone, I received Jesus Christ as my Lord and Saviour.

In a moment of time, Jean shared a word, an opportunity and a witness with me that have forever changed my life. I will never be the same because she did not withhold what she had. The love of God was in her heart and even though I did not think much of her, she saw my pitiful state and had compassion for me. I am eternally grateful for Jean's heart to share and pray that being strengthened through the grace of God, as I have been shown compassion, I will resist the temptation to judge and ultimately withhold a word, an opportunity or a witness to anyone.

Sharing promotes relationship because it requires us to give of what we have, demonstrates compassion to those who are in need, and reminds us of the spiritual connection we have with God and our brothers and sisters in the Body of Christ. Most significantly, sharing is essential to inviting those who are not a part of the Body of Christ into the family of God.

Love Compels One to Share! Love Accepts Correction and Welcomes Reproof!

PART THREE

Pocket Pearls And The "Nevers"

Pocket Pearls and the "Nevers"

My mother was a wonderful woman. As is the case with most children, I did not appreciate who she was as a mother because of her many rules, whippings (spankings), dos and don'ts and "nevers." I did not understand how and why I and my siblings were made to say 'yes ma'am' and 'no sir'; to be polite to others by always speaking first; to never speak out of turn; to never accept food when visiting friends, even if we were hungry; and to stay on the porch (in the summer) or come in the house (in the winter) once the street lights came on. My life seemed to be filled with a myriad of rules telling me what to do, what not to do, and what was never to be done. What I realize now is that my mother's words were filled with wisdom and experience that I would need in order to become the woman that I am.

With all of the dos and don'ts and "nevers," there were two things my mother expressed to my siblings and me that were at the top on the list of "nevers." I can envision her stern yet compassionate gaze as she told us that we must "never forget her birthday and never put her in a nursing home." Of course, we nervously laughed and promised to abide by these very important "nevers." We never forgot her birthday and always had some form of celebration. Throughout her life, we had "Mollie" birthday celebrations at her house, in our homes, and in restaurants within a 10-mile radius of her home. She was picky about what and where she ate. As I remember, the celebrations for my mother's birthdays always included gifts. I really think that was the most significant part of acknowledging the birthday. But, as she grew older, I began to sense that it wasn't just the gifts, my mother's "never" was given to us so that we would always be near her. It might have started as a way of getting attention and gifts (I can see her opening cards without reading a single word and shaking them for contents). We honored her wish to never forget her birthday and I believe that this provided a level of fulfillment in her life that we will never be able to understand.

In the years preceding my mother's death, she was very sick and required round-the-clock care towards the end of her life. My sisters and I did everything we could to honor her "never" with respect to being in a nursing home. We made schedules and obtained help to care for her at home. We pleaded with her to live with one of us, knowing that what she really wanted was to be near her family. Even in our best efforts, her failing health required that she spend a considerable amount of time in a rehabilitation facility; the thing she feared most. While we could not honor this "never" in the way my mother wanted, I believe that the intent of the "never" was realized. My siblings and I made sure that my mother was never alone.

Never is a very strong and definite word. When applied to the elimination of destructive habits or behaviors that undermine achievement of spiritual and natural goals, the word provides a positive force for change. Paradoxically, the limitations of our humanity make it almost impossible to stick to a "never." During my first year in college, I committed to never eating meat again. My commitment was easily compromised during the first cookout of summer break. In recalling that incident, I realize that determining to include a "never" in one's life is a very serious thing. I am sure that there are many "nevers" we have not kept, or will not be able to keep, because we are limited by our human frailty. As great as the determination may be and as strong as the desire burns within us to make a "never" a reality, human nature and an unwilling flesh tend to test and ultimately destroy many of our "nevers." There are also times when external forces, beyond our knowledge and beyond our control over them, present a pressure against which we are unable to stand. In these instances, even the greatest commitment to never do something is challenged and finally broken by these forces, leaving behind an unrealized "never." In order to maintain the "nevers" in our lives, we need a power beyond will power and a clear understanding of the significance of the "never" as a part of one's life.

The following Pearls begin with the word never. According to Webster's Dictionary, "never" means "not ever, at no time, not in any degree, and not under any condition."[11] These "nevers" are intended to encourage you to **not ever, at any time, not in any degree and under any condition fear who God made you to be**, **fear to speak the truth in love** or **fear the person of man**.

Chapter Eleven

Pearl Ten:
Never Fear the You that God Made You to Be!

For thou hast possessed my reins: thou has covered me in my mother's womb. I will praise thee; for I am fearfully and wonderfully made: marvelous are thy works; and that my soul knoweth right well. My substance was not hid from thee, when I was made in secret, and curiously wrought in the lowest parts of the earth (Psalm 139:13-15).

As the oldest of seven children, I was consistently given responsibility to watch over and lead my siblings. As a result, I suffered quite a bit of ridicule at the hands of my brothers and sisters. Sibling rivalry, resistance to household rules and chores, and of course, the age-old "you're not the boss of me" syndrome were the daily forces challenging my childhood leadership. Needless to say, I often found myself trying to recover from the wounds of being an "outcast."

I remember when I was at the age where my parents could trust me to help them secure a place for "Santa's toys." For me, guarding the goods was a serious job. In remembering my parents' efforts, I am warmed inside by the thought of the sacrifices they made to ensure that our childhood was filled with all of the things that reflected their love and care for us. I understood it to be my duty as the older sister to aid in my parents' desire to protect the wonder of Christmas in the hearts of my younger siblings. Of course, my leadership was very much challenged when one of them found the toys that my parents had so carefully hidden. Once I figured out that they had found the toys long before Christmas, I thought it my duty and responsibility to tell my mother. As you probably know, that did not go over well with the tribe. Not only did they call me names and promise never to tell me anything ever again, they also told their neighborhood friends, which meant that there were people (little people) outside of our family who disdained my leadership.

I am sure that experiences like those helped to shape my thoughts concerning who I was as a child and who I would become as an adult. I wanted to be the leader my parents could trust but I also wanted to be the sister that my siblings would talk to and hang out with. My siblings' feelings about me were important because my parents always told us that we were to love each other and "stay together." My parents taught us the value of togetherness; however, in the midst of it, my feelings of inadequacy as a favorite sister to my siblings were quite difficult to overcome. I would always be the eldest and they would always (the time seems that long when you are young) be the younger recipients of my oversight and leadership.

The hierarchy of leadership in a family changes rapidly as children grow and leave the nest. When I went away to college, my siblings adjusted to leadership from my sister under me. When I returned home during the summer, I was moved out of the bedroom that I had shared with her. In addition to the logistical changes, my siblings were not up to having me tell them what to do.

Not only did my status as an older sister and the response of unhappy siblings create a question in my mind as to my worth and value, growing up, many things contributed to this question of my worth. Several aspects of my body just didn't seem to be "like" my other siblings or the pretty people in my sphere of influence. I thought my sister had the nicest hair — it was long, thick, and curly. By contrast, mine was short and nappy. I hated my hair.

In my mind, I was also darker than any other person I knew. I am sure that this was not the case; however, it seemed so to me. I will never forget the day I was sent to the corner store (about a quarter of a mile) near my house to get something for my mother. Typically, a trip to the corner store meant that one of my siblings, if not all, would accompany me. On this day, I was alone and somewhat afraid, although I had made that trip countless times. As I was nearing the store, a little boy who was shorter and smaller than I approached me saying "hey blackie, what'cha know blackie." Behind his back, he had a small rock that he proceeded to throw right into my forehead. After throwing the rock, he ran laughing calling me blackie the entire time.

I was scared, hurt, and crushed. I went on to the store shaking like a leaf. By the time I got home, I told my mother what had happened. There was not much that she could do. Once she inspected the site of the injury and found it to be unscarred, I think she might have said something like, "don't listen when someone calls you out of your name." In my mind, this was her way of saying you are not what they said and what they said is not true — you are beautiful and I love you. Now, these words did not come from her lips; rather, they were the sum total of my understanding of how my mother and father regarded me. They loved me for who I was and in their eyes, I was beautiful — at least two people thought so. This was my understanding as long as I was at home. The problem was that I was not going to live at home forever; there would be countless trips to stores, schools, and places where I could only see myself as a skinny girl with coal black skin, short nappy hair, glasses and big teeth.

A few days after the incident on the way to the store, I saw the little boy who had hit me. He was coming down the stairs of my school. I was too afraid to say anything and too embarrassed to tell anyone else about what happened. It wasn't the fact that he had hit me in the head with a rock that caused my hurt. It was the fact that he had said out loud what I had feared for so long; that I was too black to be regarded as pretty.

As a result of this and other words spoken by family, friends, teachers and many other people in my sphere of influence growing up, I did not think very much of myself. I was very smart, mostly a straight A student, and I had a loving and supportive family (immediate and extended). But, the way I saw myself was extracted from intentional negative words and attitudes. At other times, those cutting remarks were just an insignificant part of jokes and teasing common to growing up in the city. Either way, my perception of myself was marred by words and experiences that did not allow me to grow up thinking about myself in the way God saw me.

It is almost baffling how simple words can make their way into a child's head and become embedded in the very core of who he or she might become. My inappropriate regard for myself was evident as I hated taking pictures, smiled with my hand covering my mouth (I thought my teeth were too big for my head), and thought that no man would ever love me as a wife. I just saw myself as ugly, unattractive and destined to be forgotten. As I grew older, I did not say it but that central thought permeated practically everything I did in life. The one thing I was confident about was my intellect. I did not have to prove this to anyone except my teachers and my parents. They were delighted by it, told me that I was smart and encouraged me along the way. As a matter of fact, my father always reminded us that there was "no such thing as a dumb Oliver" (my maiden name). While growing up, I don't remember anyone calling me pretty but I remember my father telling me that I was smart.

Negative experiences and destructive words can cause one to shrink back with low self-esteem or project forward with unbridled arrogance. When this happens, it is possibly an indication of intimidation or fear of being who God made us to be.

The scripture reference for this Pearl is a part of the Psalms. Psalm 139 is, for me, a most inspiring and yet challenging portion of Scripture. I run to it when I have crushed myself in self-doubt, questioned my value, and have misgivings about my worth. Verse 14 says, *"I will praise thee; for I am fearfully and wonderfully made: marvelous are thy works; and that my soul knoweth right well."* What is necessary to recognize in this verse is that the first four words, I will praise thee, reflect the response that every human being should express when considering their existence. The Hebrew translation of those four words is, *"let me praise You,"* which suggests that any consideration of who we are as a creation of God warrants an insistence to praise Him — to thank the Creator of the universe for allowing His creation in human form to exist in time and space as we do. He has made us and that is enough! No matter my feelings and fears about *what* He has made, He has made me to be exactly *who I am*. There was no mistake, and the conditions, circumstances and experiences of my existence are inconsequential to His omniscience, His omnipresence and His omnipotence. He is an all-knowing, always present and all-powerful God who wanted me to be me!

Of course, when considering one's existence, it is often easy to think about human characteristics that we compare or measure against those in the world around us. When we do this, there is a tendency to allow the comparison and the desire to measure up to what we think is good or right to cause us to question our worth and value. This is where fear and doubt of the miraculous and magnificent work of God can begin to creep into our thoughts and ultimately affect our actions. It is easy for us to be intimidated by the possibility that we are not all that we need to be, or we can shrink back in fear of continuing to be "less than" in a "better than" world.

Verse 14 in Psalm 139 also includes two words that should help us to see beyond intimidation and fear of who God made us. It says that we are "fearfully" and "wonderfully" made. One Hebrew translation of being fearfully and wonderfully made is, *"with wonders I have been distinguished."* Think of it! The writer expresses a sentiment that must fill the soul with awe and praise at the same time. My very existence is a miracle, a wonder that cannot be taken for granted or lightly. Verses 13 says, *"For thou has possessed my reins: thou has covered me in my mother's womb."* That our reins (our whole being) were possessed means that before we could know God, He knew us. As Charles Spurgeon states, "He hid us away as a treasure until He saw fit to bring us into the light of day."[12] This speaks to the intimacy God had with each of us before we were born. The word "covered" in the second part of the verse means to interweave or to knit together. We were woven or put together in our mother's womb. Verse 15 tells us that in our most secret condition, before physical birth, we were woven together to become a rendition of the miraculous work of a Holy God while constantly under His control and guardianship.

How unspeakable and incomprehensible is the wonder of our existence. The Psalmist begins by exclaiming that the knowledge of how God knew us before we were created and formed, hid us until the proper time, brought us into the world in the fullness of time, and daily knows and monitors every thought before we can even think it is beyond one's ability to even ponder. It is no wonder the Psalmist insisted on praising God for his existence. You and I are miracles to behold. God created the universe; this planet on which we live and all others, known and unknown. He created every living creature, seen and unseen. In all of His creation, there is nothing that can compare to His creation, man. This is what verse 14 means when it says we are wonderfully made — we are distinguished from all creation.

Knowing that God is the Source of our lives, having created and formed us and having distinguished us for a relationship with Him should cause us to accept ourselves, appreciate what God has made, and determine to live in a manner that consistently reflects that appreciation. But there are many people who cannot and will not appreciate the miracle God has wrought by bringing them into the world. I know, I was one of them. On the other hand, there are those who have mistaken being fearfully and wonderfully made for an opportunity to be self-focused, self-projecting and self-sustaining. Whether they realize it or not, they, in ignorance, fear who they are because they do not acknowledge and accept themselves as God's divine creation.

When we do not acknowledge or accept who we are as a creation of God, we, in essence, automatically acknowledge our existence as self-perpetuated. Our approach to life is to do things based on what appears necessary to protect, promote, and provide for ourselves. This way of thinking can blossom very quickly and take the form of a disregard for others and, ultimately, for human life. I believe it is what causes someone to have no problem with taking a life.

Regardless of the magnitude of this way of thinking, it is necessary to deal with it immediately once recognized. That is why I believe the Psalmist said, "let me praise You" when he realized that he in no way controlled or could have controlled his existence. The writer of the Psalms recognized that a relationship with his Creator had been started long before he knew it. The writer also knew that it was that relationship that would be necessary to sustain his existence.

If we have not fully acknowledged and accepted God as the Source and Sustainer of our existence, I believe there are three "selfisms" that may be at work in our lives.

A selfism is the system of belief, doctrine or theory that one holds concerning himself or herself. These three selfisms have a negative influence because they result in behaviors and actions that are contrary to the Word of God. It is possible that one or all of these selfisms will be at work at any given time. They are dangerous because they prevent an effective relationship with God and others. The first selfism is **self-dependence.** This selfism arises when we trust our own intellect and understanding for dealing with and addressing the circumstances and situations of daily living. It arises when one fails to acknowledge God as the Source and Sustainer of one's existence and that there is an answer for every life situation in His Word. This selfism is really what the Bible calls "leaning to our own understanding" (Proverbs 3:5). The danger in leaning to one's own understanding is that we neglect and ultimately refuse the wisdom of God, which is found in His Word. In John 5:30, Jesus said *"I am able to do nothing from Myself [independently, of My own accord — but only as I am taught by God and as I get His orders]. Even as I hear, I judge [I decide as I am bidden to decide. As the voice comes, to Me, so I give a decision], and My judgment is right (just, righteous), because I do not seek or consult My own will [I have no desire to do what is pleasing to Myself, My own aim, My own purpose] but only the will and pleasure of the Father Who* *sent Me" (Amplified Version).* This verse of scripture speaks to Jesus' total surrender to the will of the Father. In His submission, He acknowledged the Father as the Source and Sustainer of His life. Leaning to one's own understanding is also dangerous because we tend to deal with and respond to others based on this understanding. When this happens, we prescribe our understanding to others with an expectation that they will adopt it as their own. When they do not, we become judgmental, impatient and often frustrated with those to whom and for whom the understanding was given. Self-dependence keeps us from trusting God and trusting others. It locks us in a prison of pride, insecurity and blame that can only be opened with acknowledging and accepting God as the Source and Sustainer of our existence.

The second selfism that blocks our ability to acknowledge and accept God as our Creator is **self-distress.** We live in a world where our minds are bombarded with bits of information every second. Even when we go to sleep, remnants of the day's information continue to swirl through our minds. This sometimes happens so frequently that many experience sleeplessness as a normal occurrence, necessitating prescription and over-the-counter remedies. I noticed recently that there are more "sleep helpers" available than ever before. Many people need help to turn off the noise of life to simply get a good night's sleep. The more we allow the facts, figures, words, gossip, tweets, games, noise, images, pictures, letters, numbers, and the myriad of bits of information to enter our mind space, the greater the potential for self-distress. It is caused by an imbalance between external information and internal wisdom, and it begins when we hand over control of the mind space to the incoming information and neglect the presence of the Creator of our existence. Self-distress keeps us from considering God and considering others. We have difficulty giving ourselves in a real relationship with God and viable relationships with others. It forces us to stress, creating distress or worry that stems from regret for past mistakes and missed opportunities and fear and dread of the future. When we fully acknowledge and accept the Creator of our existence, we can cast the whole of our cares on Him because He cares for us (1 Peter 5:7).

The third selfism that may block our ability to acknowledge and accept God as the Creator of our existence is **self-deceit**. This selfism presents a very serious danger to Christians because it causes them to believe that they are "okay" apart from a **real** relationship with God. This selfism occurs after a prolonged period of living in self-dependence. People living in self-deceit have a mindset that says where they came from and where they are going (before birth and after death) does not figure into how they may be living life today. They are happy when things are going the way they want, and they are in the pits when life is just not working. Most of their life accomplishments center upon their effort, ability and endeavors. When things are totally out of kilter (finances, relationships, etc.), they further deceive themselves by thinking that one more self-directed or self-prescribed approach will turn things around. They are unwilling to stop, settle and be still long enough to acknowledge that they need help from a Source greater than themselves. Self-deceit keeps us from accepting the truth from God and from others. Like self-distress, it locks us in a prison of pride that will, unless addressed early and effectively, damage our credibility and stain our character. When we acknowledge that God is the Source and Sustainer of our lives, we no longer deceive ourselves into thinking that people, places or things can sustain us and make us happy. We learn and appreciate I John 2:17, which says *"And the world passes away and disappears, and with it the forbidden cravings (the passionate desires, the lust) of it; but he who does the will of God and carries out His purposes in his life abides (remains) forever"* (Amplified Version).

The aforementioned selfisms must be addressed. In many instances, they exist for so long in those who have not accepted Jesus Christ as Saviour that they lead many to reprobation. Thus, it is important for non-Christians to address these sooner than later. Christians, too, must be quick to deal with these selfisms.

The previously discussed selfisms occur when we do not fully acknowledge and accept God as the Source and Sustainer of our lives. However, when we do acknowledge and accept God as the Source and Sustainer of our lives, there are two selfisms reflected in this Pearl. They are **self-respect** and **self-appreciation**. The word respect means, esteem, regard, or reverence. When we have self-respect, we regard, esteem or reverence who we are as a creation of God. To appreciate means to value or admire. When we have self-appreciation, it means we value and admire who we are as a creation of God. These two selfisms are essential and necessary because they help diminish and ultimately destroy self-dependence, self-distress and self-deceit. When these are destroyed and self-respect and self-appreciation govern, then and only then can God use our lives to bring glory and honor to His name. God has fearfully made us and distinguished us from all of His creation. His desire is that we acknowledge and accept His place in our lives as Source and Sustainer. When we do this we gain the proper sense of self because we acknowledge Who He is and accept how He has made us. This leads to a sense of respect for who God made us - we respect ourselves. This should bring about a sense of appreciation for who we are - we appreciate ourselves.

Never Fear the You that God Made You to Be!

Chapter Twelve

Pearl Eleven:
Never Be Afraid to Share What You Think. In Your Thoughts are Hidden Gems for the Growth of Others and Rods for the Correction of Self!

Therefore, though I have abundant bold-ness in Christ to charge you to do what is fitting and required and your duty to do, Yet for love's sake I prefer to appeal to you just for what I am — I, Paul, an ambassador [of Christ Jesus] and an old man and now a prisoner for His sake... (Philemon 8-9, Amplified Version).

I remember a statement from years ago that I heard on television, in my family circle, and just about anywhere where someone wanted to let someone else know just what they were thinking. The statement was "I am going to give them a piece of my mind." In subsequent years, I remember a joke about those words that implied if one kept giving away pieces of one's mind, soon there would be nothing left. It does not appear possible that there are those who have exhausted their storehouse of thoughts or pieces of their minds. In this day and time, practically everyone has an opinion, an idea, a recommendation, a perspective, and/or a suggestion. The Internet, particularly social media, has created a platform whereby anyone with a computer or a phone and a data plan can give away pieces of the mind in a millisecond. There seems to be a never-ending supply of thoughts and words flowing in the atmosphere. No one seems to be afraid to share them. The problem is, often, a lot of what is being said adds to an overabundance of information, creating information overload. In daily sorting through the countless e-mails, advertisements, infomercials, and many other conduits that bring information my way, I have found that a great deal of the information does not add much to my spiritual, mental, and/or social well-being. This causes me to consider my own words and the information I give each day. In an age of information overload, I have learned that my words can be helpful and, if not filtered through a heart of love, they can be harmful. I must consider my words and speak the truth in love.

The world in which we live is saturated with information. This saturation is perpetuated by an instantaneous connectivity that makes it all readily available. Therefore, it is often difficult to ascertain what to believe of information received. It is also hard, at times, to know what to say when desiring to give information. When received, information has to be dealt with. The moment it enters the mind, something must be done to process it and determine a response of some kind. Whether we are present to observe a verbal or nonverbal response to what we give in the way of information, when we are the source of information, our words to the listener require and generate a response.

This Pearl is an encouragement to consider and then filter our words; knowing that as they are received, they will undoubtedly influence those to whom they are given. Because words are often the medium through which information reaches the mind of those with whom we communicate, it is important for Christians to speak the truth in love. That is, we must ensure that our communication, whether words or deeds, is presented through the truth of God's Word and with love. Speaking the truth in love is a simple yet profound admonishment that is presented in one way or another throughout the New Testament. It is specifically stated in Ephesians chapter 4. In this epistle, the Apostle Paul speaks to believers in the church at Ephesus about unity of the church and the purpose of the perfecting gifts in the church. In verses 11-14, he encourages believers to allow unity and the preaching of the Word of God to "grow them up" so that they would become mature Christians. As mature Christians, they could live according to Ephesians 4:15 (Amplified Version) which says, *"Rather, let our lives lovingly express truth [in all things, speaking truly, dealing truly, living truly]. Enfolded in love, let us grow up in every way and in all things into Him Who is the Head, [even] Christ (the Messiah, the Anointed One)."* This verse is a description of the mature Christian's life and lifestyle. It is also an admonishment to be ready and willing to speak truthfully out of a heart of love.

This Pearl causes me to once again think about my husband's unusual and inspiring ability to listen and respond lovingly with the truth. At his passing, he was completing a Masters degree in Counseling Psychology. I had to petition the University from which he was to receive his degree to grant it posthumously. At first I was told that it would be impossible for my husband's degree to be granted because, at the time of his death, he had two more courses to complete and granting a degree to him would set precedence since the state had never done so before. As a result, I set forth on a campaign to petition anyone who might have had any authority, clout or influence to help me to honor him and the work that he had so faithfully put into completing his degree.

After numerous letters, phone calls, and of course, unceasing prayers, the University made a decision to grant my husband's degree. One of the essential things that contributed to their agreement to do so was the letters and requests to the University that came from the people with whom and the organizations with which my husband worked in counseling. He completed the majority of his counseling hours with youth and young adults who had been placed in detention centers, special programs and school settings designed to help them to change their behaviors. Many of the youth's parents wrote letters and gave testimony of how effective my husband's counsel had been in helping their children to turn their lives around. I remember speaking to one mother who said that her son sobbed when he found out that my husband had died. She stated that no one had been able to get her son to amend his ways until my husband spent time with him and listened. Once he listened, it was the counsel her young son received that helped him to turn his life around.

My husband was a great listener but his great ability to listen was an instrumental aspect of his ability to respond to what was being said. He listened intently and then he spoke with wisdom and caring that reflected understanding and empathy. He listened to hear the "words behind the words" spoken. Once he did this, he was able to respond with words that captured and then nurtured what was presented. He was never afraid to say what he thought after having heard the heart of the speaker. He spoke the truth in love.

The scripture reference for this Pearl is taken from the book of Philemon, a one-chapter private letter from the Apostle Paul to a slave owner. The purpose of the letter was two-fold. First, Paul wanted to encourage and thank Philemon for his faithfulness in serving the Lord Jesus Christ. The testimony of Philemon's Christian life was that he lived in a way that his relationship with the Lord and his relationship with man were commendable.

The second thing Paul did in the letter was to present a humble yet passionate plea for the acceptance and restoration of Onesimus, Philemon's runaway slave. In verses eight and nine of the letter, Paul appeals to Philemon not from a position of authority as an Apostle but as a friend and brother. He appealed to Philemon out of the love of Christ — a love that was in Philemon and the same love that now abided in the heart of Onesimus, his slave. Paul shared that Onesimus had had a true conversion as Paul had ministered to him and he was confident of his salvation. Paul's plea to Philemon presents a tender yet convincing picture of the power of the love of God and how beautifully it changes our hearts and compels us to speak the truth in love. Writers suggest that Paul's plea has "a balance of conviction and compassion — conviction about the worth of Onesimus, a slave become a

Christian; and tender compassion for Philemon and the dilemma of a slave-master become a Christian."[13] Certainly, as Philemon's friend and pastor, Paul loved and respected their relationship. However, as the one who preached salvation and witnessed Onesimus' conversion to Christ, Paul greatly desired to see him restored in his relationship with his master now that he was free from the bondage of sin. The relationship would be the same, Philemon would still be the slave-master and Onesimus would still be his slave. What was different and what would make the relationship greater is that because both of them were now Christians, they would both have to demonstrate the same unconditional love toward each other that God had shown to them. This is indeed a paradox that only the love of God through Jesus Christ can answer.

Paul's position in this situation clearly points to the necessity of this Pearl. We must never be afraid to share what we think when what needs to be shared is the truth of God's Word. The context of Paul's responsibility as preacher required him to lead both slaves and the slave-masters to a saving relationship with God through Jesus Christ. In this instance, he could not allow Onesimus to remain as a runaway knowing that he had to live his life truthfully as a Christian. As a Christian, Onesimus was to live according to Ephesians 6:5-8 which says, *"Servants, be obedient to them that are your masters according to the flesh, with fear and trembling, in singleness of your heart, as unto Christ; Not with eyeservice, as menpleasers; but as the servants of Christ, doing the will of God from the heart; With good will doing service, as to the Lord, and not to men: Knowing that whatsoever good thing any man doeth, the same shall he receive of the Lord, whether he be bond or free."* In the same way, Philemon had to accept Onesimus and treat him according to Ephesians 6:9 which says, *"And, ye masters, do the same things unto them, forbearing threatening: knowing that your Master also is in heaven; neither is there respect of persons with Him.* Paul entreated Philemon boldly and without reservation because he himself had experienced the power of God's love. Having experienced God's love and forgiveness for his sinful state, Paul was compelled to continue to share love and speak the truth in love. Before Paul's conversion experience, he was bold in saying what he thought, even though it was in direct contradiction to the truth of God's Word. But, he was miraculously and eternally changed through the power of God's love. His bold transparency in speaking with Philemon was indicative of the love and correction he had received directly from the Lord.

And so it must be for every Christian. Because God loves us, He corrects us. He points to the things that are incorrect in our hearts and lives and points us in the direction we must go to please Him. When we please Him, we can have a good relationship with Him and with others. Once we have been corrected or changed by God's love, we are compelled to speak the truth in love.

Paul's letter to Philemon on behalf of Onesimus presents two areas that should be considered for sharing or communicating what you think. The first consideration is the *context.*

Anytime we want to share what we think (the truth in love), the context or atmosphere for sharing must be set with thanksgiving for the one with whom we are sharing. Paul did not begin the letter to Philemon without first recognizing what the love of God had accomplished in his dear friend's heart. He first encouraged and uplifted him. I think this was a direct result of Paul's reflection on the rods of correction that he had received through the mercy and grace of God. Being thankful for another's walk with the Lord, at any level, should always be present in our sharing. Because we do not always know the intimacies of a person's relationship with the Lord and what brought them to that relationship, the only way the truth can be deposited is by remembering that it took the same love from God to bring us into right relationship with God and others.

The second consideration is the **condition**. Our sharing of the truth in love must be based on the condition of others and not our personal or selfish desires. This helps the one who speaks the truth in love to demonstrate true concern for the recipient. Although Paul was trying to get Philemon to accept his runaway slave back into service as a brother beloved, his motives for appealing to Philemon were not self-serving. Rather, he was motivated by love for both Philemon and Onesimus. In verses 8 and 9, he indicates that he could have used his authority as an apostle to require Philemon to change his position. While this would have been right given Paul's authority and Onesimus' condition (the need for restoration), the focus would have been on Paul's position of authority to require change and Philemon's position of authority to make a change. Paul also indicated in verse 13 that he could have kept Onesimus with him because he had been a good servant to him while he (Paul) was in prison.

What was necessary for Paul to speak the truth in love was a focus on Philemon's condition. Whatever his condition, Paul did not present his authority, his friendship with Philemon, or his personal need for Onesimus' help as the focus for change. He considered Philemon's condition; a heart desiring to please God yet challenged by the prevailing circumstances of life. In so doing, his approach addressed the all-encompassing power of the love of God to change us and help us to do what is right.

The prerequisite for sharing the truth in love is that the conditions for the sharing are understood as being outside of one's own interest or ability to enforce that interest in any way. Excluding selfish desires or gain from the condition for which the truth is being given affords the speaker of the truth an opportunity to present the unconditional nature of God's love. It is only then that sharing what we think reflects a genuine concern for the person to whom we speak.

Pearl Ten says that we should not be afraid to share what we think, but it also tells us why sharing what we think (the truth in love) is necessary. First, sharing the truth in love provides "hidden gems for the growth of others." This is probably one of the greatest aspects of my husband's ability as a preacher and a counselor. Because he could listen so intently and because his humble nature allowed him to consider the condition of the person with whom he was speaking, his counsel was well received. Also, his faith in the power of the Word of God to make a difference in anyone's life was the foundation for his counsel. When he spoke the truth in love, the listener received "hidden gems" that came from the heart of God through a yielded vessel. My husband often said that he did what he did and lived the way he lived because of the grace of God working in him. This is essential to speaking the truth in love. In order to speak the truth in love, we must humble ourselves with an ever present knowing that we are what we are because of grace — the omnipotent power of God working in us and with us. Our words do not change people; only God can go to the heart of a person to help them to see how much they need the

Word of God. Only God can cause someone to hear and receive counsel from someone who speaks the truth in love.

Once we receive the truth from God allowing His Word to penetrate our hearts leading us into a life and lifestyle of love, it is virtually impossible not to share the truth because of that love. We can never know the extent to which the truth spoken in love will provide rare and precious direction, assistance, help, encouragement, support and so many gems that others may never find without hearing and receiving it. That is why they are called "hidden gems." Until the truth is spoken to someone who does not have it, it is a hidden gem. In a world where selfishness and self-centeredness abound, there are many who are searching for gems that are stored in the heart of believers who have been changed by the power of God's love.

The second thing that sharing what we think (speaking the truth in love) provides is rods for the correction of self. In the Old Testament, the Bible refers to natural instruments of chastisement and correction as rods. In New Testament times, we refer to the Word of God as the rod of correction because it is the source of chastisement and correction that helps us to grow up as children of God. Correction through the truth of God's Word is an aspect of one's personal relationship with the Lord. It is a part of the daily and purposeful steps we take to draw closer to Him (James 4:8). As we grow in our relationship with Him,

His correction allows us to become more like Him with a greater capacity to love and serve others. When we speak the truth in love, we reflect the cleansing that has taken place on the inside of us through the relationship with Him, and we are at once reminded of the rods of correction that were used to change us.

I encourage you to read that one chapter of the book of Philemon. It is beautiful, convicting and can transform the way we think about God's love and our responsibility to share the truth in love. Once we have experienced the joy and peace of a relationship with the Father that corrects through love and compels us to share the truth in love, we become instruments of hidden gems and are ever mindful of how love has changed us.

Never Be Afraid to Speak the Truth in Love!

(In your thoughts are hidden gems for the growth of others and rods for the correction of self!)

Chapter Thirteen

Pearl Twelve:
Never Fear the Person of Man!
Intimidation Due to a Man's Person
Dishonors God!

For God hath not given us a spirit of fear; but of power, and love, and of a sound mind (2 Timothy 1:7).

ear sparked by intimidation is dangerous. I experienced the devastating effect of fear as a college student. I had decided that I wanted to be a doctor long before high school and completed my school years with honors. I was prepared to go off to college and become a doctor. Once I finished high school, I entered my undergraduate studies in an honors program. As a pre-med student, I found myself trying to swim against the strong current of academic challenges, cultural differences, and unknown forces that seemed to have been established to cause me to fail. The honors program was rigorous and many of the students who were a part of it had attended high schools with much better programs and resources than mine. It was 1972 and racial discrimination was prevalent. I was among only a small number of African-American students in the pre-med program. In addition to the rigor of the program and the racial tension, there was fierce competition for coveted spaces in medical schools. Students in the program were waging a serious battle to finish at the top of the class in order to get into medical school and become doctors.

We all had the same goal but some of us were challenged with fear sparked and fueled by intimidation from our peers, the setting, and most especially, the professors. I was that student. In my naivety, I thought that I would meet fellow students who would share their experiences so that we could help each other to succeed. I also thought that the professors were there to not only provide instruction, but encouragement to help all of us to reach the goal - becoming great doctors. I was wrong and very afraid.

Fear had gripped and choked the courage that I had worked so hard for so many years to develop. The one thing that I knew I had going for me was my intelligence. This was where my courage was strong. I was quick to respond to a professor's questions and I thrived on reading and research. This aspect of confidence in who I was intellectually was also present when I met my husband. While intelligence was my courage point in high school, it was about to be shaken as I began the summer program.

While in the introductory meeting for the pre-med program, I was introduced to a professor who was responsible for overseeing the new pre-med students. I will never forget the Saturday morning we all met in a large, rather chilly room filled with faces that I did not know. Thankfully, the one familiar face in the room was a cheerful, short, round-faced girl named Marilyn who had an infectious smile and real hearty laugh. She did not look like she was afraid or intimidated at all. As a matter of fact, she looked like she was ready to do battle against any foe that would even attempt to keep her from reaching the goal. The professor said many things that day, but the one thing I remember him saying was "most of you will not make it through to medical school." Those were the words that wrapped themselves around my mind, plunged deep into my heart, and brought huge yet unreleased tears to my eyes. I was hurt and speechless as I began to try to process my feelings and my future based on what I had just heard. I was intimidated before the program started. This man had grabbed my courage without knowing it or me.

My newfound friend Marilyn did not seem moved at all by the professor's words. She was busy writing and taking in all the instructions that were given so that she could begin the process of becoming a doctor. She said, "He can't tell me what will happen." She even tried to help me see that the professor's words were just words and that the goal was attainable and reachable, not just for the students who had enjoyed a greater and more promising journey to college, but for two teenage girls who had grown up with similar lives. She was not afraid and did not let intimidation due to a man's person cause her to shrink back or give up on what she knew to be her destiny. Man did not at all intimidate her. In fact, Marilyn was never deterred or intimidated by what was said to her during that first day of the pre-med program. She did not graduate from the pre-med program; rather, she completed all of the requirements in three years and went directly to medical school. In addition to her academic success, Marilyn met and married the love of her life in medical school. She and her husband have had a very successful medical practice for more than 30 years. She did not allow fear to alter the course of her life.

As much as I tried to move beyond the intimidation of a professor's few words, I graduated college having completed a significant set of courses that would have probably gotten me into medical school. But, I allowed a seed of intimidation to become a root of fear that haunted me throughout my undergraduate experience. I changed my major in my junior year; which meant that I had to spend an additional semester in order to graduate. Even after graduation, I took two physics courses, an organic chemistry course, and a biochemistry course; trying to reclaim courage for applying to and completing medical school. I was even accepted in a special program with a major medical/dental school in my area. In that program, I was once again faced with competing against students who had finished in the top of their classes in pre-med programs across the country. In our initial meetings, we were told that only a certain few would be eligible to go directly into the university's medical/dental school program. The same fear that had gripped me in the undergraduate program took hold of me once again. One would think that after graduating with a degree that qualified me to compete for a medical school slot, I would have understood that intimidation did not have to be accepted or internalized. Its source is insignificant because it is a product of perception. I am intimidated when I think or believe that I am. The person or persons I consider the source of the intimidation may or may not be aware of my feelings and fears. I finished the program but did not get into medical school. Once again, I was intimidated without reason or cause.

Even though I went on to successfully complete graduate school, for years after my undergraduate experiences, I could sense those feelings of fear of rejection and fear of failure.The initial seed of intimidation that I had allowed to be planted in my mind by one man's words affected the course of my life. After two years of fear-filled attempts to complete the pre-med program, I switched majors to speech pathology. The blessing was that because speech pathology has an emphasis on the anatomy of the head and neck, some of the courses that I had taken as a pre-med student had the same content. In addition, I had taken several psychology classes in the pre-med program. Most, if not all, of these classes were required for the speech pathology major. It happened that this was a good transition because I ultimately graduated and went on to complete a graduate degree in communication sciences. It was during my first year in graduate school that I gave my heart completely to the Lord. While in graduate school, I started a Bible study in my tiny apartment, which led me to join the church in which I have served for more than 33 years now.

As I have looked back, I can see the orchestration of the Lord in my life, even in the midst of my fears. Completing my masters degree led to my first professorship at Elizabeth City State. Since then, I have had opportunities to work in higher education with other universities. The road from high school to college to graduate school was paved with fear but ultimately I believe the Lord "worked it together for my good." While I am clear that things "worked out," I am also certain that fear can be devastating if not dealt with once it is recognized. I am glad that the twists and turns that resulted from my fears were worked together for good.

When I consider the extent to which fear of man can stifle one's ability to move forward toward one's dreams and goals, I thank God for the day I gave my life wholeheartedly to the Lord. As I grew in the knowledge of the Word of God, I began to learn more about the devastation of intimidation that arises from fear of man. During our marriage, this Pearl was one that my husband constantly and consistently lived before me and preached to me. I encourage you to use it to examine your life and lifestyle to determine areas where fear has caused you to alter and possibly give up on a dream, an endeavor or a goal for which you have the necessary grace and gifts to complete. If God has given the grace and the gifts, fear cannot stop you, unless you allow it to.

The scripture reference for this Pearl is contained in Paul's admonishment to Timothy, a pastor who was trying to carry out his duties in the midst of criticism and challenges. Timothy was a young man who was sincere in his faith. Paul was persuaded of his genuineness and he knew that Timothy was a gifted young man. God had given Timothy tremendous gifts that were to be used in Christian ministry.

In 1 Timothy 4:12, Paul encourages Timothy not to allow anyone to discount his ministry because of his youth. As a young pastor, Timothy might have been somewhat intimidated by the aged or mature members of the church.

Fear in response to intimidation does not please God because it keeps the spiritual gifts and callings that God entrusts and places on the inside of man dormant and unprofitable to the Body of Christ. Romans 12 provides a description of the functional gifts; one of the three sets of spiritual gifts God gives to man. This scripture reference clearly instructs believers that God gives the gift, we have stewardship over the gift and must use them, and the gifts are given for the benefit of the entire Body of Christ. Speaking to members of the Body of Christ, Romans 12:4-6a says, *"For as in one physical body we have many parts (organs, members) and all of these parts do not have the same function or use, So we, numerous as we are, are one body in Christ (the Messiah) and individually we are parts one of another [mutually dependent on one another]. Having gifts (faculties, talents, qualities) that differ according to the grace given us, let us use them"* (Amplified Version).

Before addressing Timothy's fear, the Apostle Paul gave him one instruction that

I believe is necessary to address fear that results from intimidation by man. In 2 Timothy 1:6, Paul says, *"Wherefore I put thee in remembrance that thou stir up the gift of God, which is in thee by the putting on of my hands."* Paul was referring to the spiritual gift that Timothy had received by the grace of God to pastor and lead the church at Ephesus. As noted earlier, God gives each believer spiritual gifts for which we have stewardship and are responsible for using for the benefit of the entire Body of Christ. They are also entrusted to us and placed on the inside of us so that non-Christians can "see" the love of God manifested in how we care for and treat one another with those gifts. Spiritual gifts are essential to the work of ministry and the spreading of the Gospel.

In 2 Timothy 1:7, the reference for this Pearl, Paul told Timothy that God has not given us a spirit of fear. In this context, the word fear means lack of confidence. It is an inability to go forward in service to and for the Lord. Timothy was equipped, he had authority and there was a congregation in need of his service but he lacked confidence. It was imperative that Timothy deal with the presence of fear. The success and furtherance of God's will for the church at Ephesus depended on it.

In addition to lack of confidence, this type of fear is marked by an attitude that can cause one to stop testifying or witnessing for the Lord. Such fear is often observed as shame. Because God entrusts His gifts and callings to us, we are the agent by which His will and work can be done in the earth. When we allow fear to linger and lack of confidence in what God has done on the inside keeps us from moving forward, the tendency to shrink back or remain silent about what God has done increases. We can find ourselves in a place of cowardice and timidity with respect to sharing and demonstrating the wonderful and powerful work of grace that is evident in spiritual gifts and callings. If allowed to continue, Timothy's fear could have stifled his witness to a point where the Gospel would not have been preached. Of course, this could have destroyed the church and its effectiveness to the local community.

The solution to fear or the lack of confidence for moving forward in what God has called us to do is to "stir up" the gifts. This is what Paul told Timothy to do in 2 Timothy 1:6. The term stir up in this context means to "fan the flame." In other words, when fear grips us in a way that stymies forward movement and stunts spiritual growth, we must quickly allow the power of the Holy Spirit to help us to break free from fear's grip and allow the gifts that God has so graciously given to be made visible and usable.

The Bible says, *"the gifts and calling of God are without repentance"* (Romans 11:29). In this verse, the word gifts is the Greek word "charisma," which means "the results of grace." According to Spiros Zodhaites, it is a "gift of grace; an undeserved benefit from God."[14] God equips us with all that we need to carry out His plan and purpose. Because we cannot know how significant the gifts on the inside of us are to the salvation and spiritual growth of others, it is possible that the lives of many people are negatively affected because we are "stuck" in the grips of fear. Because God loves us and because He wants to offer salvation, eternal life, and abundant life to everyone who will receive it, He has given us gifts so that our lives will reflect His love and cause others to want what they see in us. How it must dishonor God when we allow the words and attitudes of mere men to cause us to fear and, then, refuse to do what God has called us to do. When we allow fear to permeate and then dominate our lives and lifestyle, it creates a darkness that clouds and seemingly smothers the glow of the magnificent gifts of grace that are essential to the Christian walk.

In order to stir up the gifts on the inside of us, we must allow the Holy Spirit to empower and lead us. Once we surrender to the power of the Holy Spirit, we can take three practical steps. Together, they involve mind, body and spirit under the power and influence of the Holy Spirit. First, **re-gain the proper perspective**. This involves the mind and is necessary to gain a mental focus. Fear is first perceived with the mind. Once it is planted in the mind, it can then become rooted in the thoughts and imaginations that shape our responses to life and life situations. This is the point at which fear becomes the focus of actions and reactions. In essence, it is like a bit in a horse's mouth; it controls its movement and ultimately determines where and how far it can go.

In order to stir up the gifts on the inside, it is imperative that we change our focus from fear of the person of man to faith in God's Word. I believe this is why Paul told Timothy in 2 Timothy 1:13 to "hold fast" or retain the standard that was given to him through the Word of God. Instead of focusing on the challenges and certainly the feelings and emotions (fear) that resulted from the challenges, Timothy had to hold fast to what he had been taught from the Word of God. We stir up the gifts on the inside by having a proper perspective - a mental focus on the Word of God.

Second, **practice persistence**. According to Webster's, the word practice means to perform or work at repeatedly to become proficient.[15] Webster's says, the word persistence or to persist means to go resolutely or stubbornly in spite of opposition, importunity, or warning.[16] It also means to remain unchanged or fixed in a specified character, condition or position. These two words together reflect what we do with our bodies in order to stir up the gifts. In essence, practicing persistence means developing and maintaining natural discipline.

In order to stir up the gift on the inside, we perform those actions and activities that are consistent with what the Word of God describes as useful and becoming for a Christian. These actions and activities are performed repeatedly and resolutely with an unchanged character until we are proficient in demonstrating the character of Christ and actions of love. I believe this is why in 2 Timothy chapter two, Paul admonished Timothy to study as a workman and then do the work. He was to avoid idle conversations, flee youthful lusts, and preach the truth. He had to do these things in the face of hardness, difficulty and opposition to his leadership. These were the things Timothy had to practice with persistence so that he could be "...*strong (strengthened inwardly) in the grace (spiritual blessings) that is [to be found] in Christ Jesus*" (2 Timothy 2:1 Amplified Version). We stir up the gift on the inside when we are naturally disciplined in living according to the Word of God.

Third, **put on patience**. This involves the spirit man and means to wait on the Lord. It is not an aimless, nonproductive waiting process. It means gaining a better and more specific understanding of and appreciation for the relationship that we have with the God and Father who created us. Having this kind of patience is necessary because our efforts apart from God (without the knowledge of His will) and without the assurance of His presence are empty. If we want to hear from Him, appreciate the value and significance of what He has placed on the inside of us, and realize the magnitude of His plan and purpose for our lives, we must wait on Him. We cannot be slaves to time and servants to our flesh.

For each of those three practical steps we can take to stir up the gifts on the inside, it is essential to recognize and understand that they can only be taken by the power of the Holy Spirit. Once we begin to fan the flames, it is the fire of the Holy Spirit that will fuel our resolve to cease to allow the words and attitudes of others to produce intimidation that leads to fear. As we saw in the introduction to the "nevers," a power beyond will power is necessary to effectively keep the "nevers" in our lives. Paul told Timothy in 2 Timothy 1:14 to, *"guard and keep [with the greatest care] the precious and excellently adapted [Truth] which has been entrusted [to you], by the [help of the] Holy Spirit Who makes His home in us"* (Amplified Version).

In the same manner that Paul admonished and encouraged Timothy, I encourage you. Never fear the person of man. God through grace gives us spiritual gifts that manifest in abilities and talents for service to Him. When we are intimidated and fear, a lack of confidence stifles and diminishes an effective witness for others. Ultimately, it also kills opportunities for growth and development in us.

We can eliminate the grip of fear that keeps us from allowing the precious gifts and callings that God has so graciously given by allowing the Holy Spirit to help us. He empowers us to have the mental focus, the natural discipline and patience to wait on God so that what is on the inside can bring glory and honor to the Lord.

Never Fear the Person of Man!

(Intimidation due to a man's person dishonors God)

Conclusion

Again, the kingdom of heaven is like unto a merchant man, seeking goodly pearls: Who, when he had found one pearl of great price, went and sold all that he had, and bought it (Matthew 13:45-46).

It has taken more than 15 years to write this book. In the early days after my husband's passing, I poured through his books, letters, and writings to be close to him as I missed him so very much. On most occasions, I cried and questioned the Lord as to why I had to go through such a terrible loss. My husband was an excellent writer, teacher and scholar. But what he did was not the central focus for my writing this book. It is who he was. The essence of his life in Christ has compelled me to write. Steve was not perfect, but his life reflected Christ's character in a way that changed my life and

I was compelled to share. Accordingly, this book is written not for gain, money, prestige, fame, fortune or even notoriety, but simply to help anyone needing encouragement to live a life that is pleasing to God and find the Pearl of Great Price. The simplicity and peace that are inherent in living with the Pearl of Great Price cannot be described or fully contained in a book.

After my husband died, the Pearls were tucked away in a folder with several other papers. I found them while going through things in his office while I was working toward using his office as my office. The papers were hand-written and chronicled my husband's three-day seclusion with the Lord; the occasion on which the Pearls were given to him. As I am writing this, I am looking at the twenty or so pages of a yellow legal pad with frayed edges, perfect penmanship and most importantly, words from God to my husband [to me]. Those pages included my husband's vision for ministry and several sections with my name in them. Those sections express what my part and significance were to be as a part of my husband's life and ministry. As I write this, I am in tears as I was the first time I read the masterful and magnificent "plan" God had given my husband.

The pages that accompanied the Pearls not only included God's plan for my life and my husband's life and ministry, they also included specific instructions to my husband as to what he must do to prepare for and carry out the plan. Thus, the Lord gave him the Pearls — they were essential to his growth and development and necessary for all that lay ahead.

It was the uncertainty of what lay ahead that gripped me for more than fifteen years. Even as I was experiencing the faithfulness of God and the blessings of being a Christian, every now and then, the thought and the difficult feeling of loss flooded my mind and made my heart ache. While not clear to me at the time, in subsequent years I have accepted that the plan was not limited to the 13,140 days of Steve's life. The plan continues. As my name was on those pages, I believe that my assignment as his wife and a preacher of the Gospel is to work the plan with the Pearls until I see the man to whom the plan and the Pearls were given in Heaven. For ten short years, I had to see the Pearls in Steve's life to learn them. I had to learn the Pearls in order to live them. Now, I must live the Pearls in order to continue the legacy of his life. They are the keys, the tools and the "nevers" that will help me to actualize God's plan for my life without him.

To me, the Pearls are precious beyond measure. Prayerfully, you have received them and plan on putting them to good use. I invite you to come back to them regularly, perhaps daily, in order to truly allow them to adorn your life.

Thank you for joining me on the journey of sharing these Pearls. I cannot begin to tell you how challenging and, yet, wonderful the process of putting words to these simple truths from my husband's heart has been. I have cried, I have smiled, and I have even doubted whether anyone else would be as interested and enamored by such a simple yet beautiful life. To whatever extent Pocket Pearls has influenced or spoken to your heart, I am grateful to God and appreciate you for reading them. Please share them with others. It was my husband's simple and clear way of living these Pearls that so strikingly changed me and helped me to see Jesus!

I know that it was my husband's relationship with the Lord that caused him to live these Pearls and to be the example of Christ for me. Because of his example, I have grown in my relationship with the Lord. The bottom line is that both of our lives were changed when we received Jesus Christ as Lord and Saviour and when we allowed the blessed Holy Spirit to lead, guide and direct our lives.

Because the love of God compelled us to live, love, give, have joy, serve, forgive, be honest, reject fear, and share, it is essential that we offer you what was offered to us. If you do not have a relationship with God through Jesus Christ His Son or if, after having read this book, you recognize that the relationship is not what it should be, there are three things you can do. First, get to know Him. To know God is to have a relationship with Him. We love Him because He first loved us. John 3:16 says that He loved us so much that He sent His Son to die for us so that we could have eternal life in Heaven and abundant life now. We cannot know Him with our minds; we must know Him in our hearts. To know Him requires only two simple things, invite Him into your heart, that is, ask Him to be your Saviour and ask Him to fill your heart. Tell Him that you want to have a relationship with Him so that you can experience His love, accept His help and extend love to others. The second thing you can do to know Him is to believe that your invitation was accepted and that His place in your heart is secure. Once you do these two simple things, your life will never be the same.

Second, admit you need Him. To need God is to rely on Him. Once you know Him, allow the relationship to deepen through trusting Him. In order for this to happen, rely on Him for who He is. He is the Source, the Strength, and the Sustainer of your life. Before now, it may have been difficult to grasp the idea of relinquishing the control you thought you had over your life. It is okay to surrender to the truth that you need help beyond what is humanly possible. It is okay to need God.

Once you are certain of who He is, then you can rely on Him for what He will do. What God does for us is greater than any natural or material blessing. The most essential and significant thing He does for us is to never leave us or forsake us. His presence with us ensures our peace, secures our provisions, and assures our protection. You can trust Him because you need Him.

Finally, draw near Him. To draw near to God is to run to Him. Once you begin to rely on Him, seek to be in His presence all the time. This is done through prayer, meditation, and the study of the Word of God. The Bible teaches us that when we draw near to God, He will draw near to us. This means that He is always present and wanting to get closer to you. This sweet fellowship sustains and strengthens the relationship.

Once you know Him, you will realize how much you need Him and once you realize how much you need Him, you will want to draw near Him. Now that you have taken steps to establish or strengthen your relationship with Him, use Pocket Pearls daily. They will make you wise and cause you to live a life well-pleasing to God.

Notes

1. Aaron Smith and Maeve Duggan, "Online Dating and Relationships," *Pew Research* (2014), http://pewinternet.org/Reports/2013/Online-Dating.aspx.

2. ibid., 5

3. ibid.

4. ibid.

5. Ralph Harris et al., *The New Testament Study Bible Romans-Corinthians*. (Springfield: World Library Press, Inc., 1986), 127.

6. *Webster's New Collegiate Dictionary*, s.v. "smile."

7. Fred H. Wight, *Manners and Customs of Bible Lands,* 5th ed. (Chicago: Moody Press, 1953), 69-79.

8. Spiros Zodhiates and Warren Baker, *The Hebrew-Greek Key Word Study Bible King James Version* (Revised Edition). (Chattanooga: AMG Publishers, 1991) 81.

9. Sharon Lohman, "A Brief History of Bread," *History* (2013), www.history.com/news/ hungry-history/a-brief-history-of-bread

10. Ralph Harris et al., *The New Testament Study Bible John.* (Springfield: World Library Press, Inc., 1986), 165

11. *Webster's New Collegiate Dictionary,* s.v. "never."

12. Charles Hadden Spurgen, *Psalms* (Grand Rapids: Kregel Publications, 1968), 637.

13. Lloyd Ogilvie and Maxie Dunnam, *The Communicator's Commentary* (Waco: Word Books, 1982), 412.

14. Zodhiates, *Hebrew-Greek Key Word Study Bible,* 1768.

15. *Webster's New Collegiate Dictionary,* s.v. "practice."

16. *Webster's New Collegiate Dictionary,* s.v. "persistence."

Bibliography

Harris, Ralph, Stanley M. Horton, and Gayle Garrity Seaver. *The New Testament Study Bible John.* Springfield: World Library Press, Inc., 1991.

Harris, Ralph, Stanley M. Horton, and Gayle Garrity Seaver. *The New Testament Study Bible Romans-Corinthians.* Springfield: World Library Press, Inc., 1991.

Ogilvie, Lloyd John and Maxie D. Dunnam, eds. *The Communicator's Commentary.* Waco: Word Books, 1982.

Spurgeon, Charles Hadden. *Psalms.* Grand Rapids: Kregel Publications, 1968.

Webster's New Collegiate Dictionary. Springfield: G. and C. Merriam Company, 1975.

Wright, Fred H. *Manners and Customs of Bible Lands.* 5th ed. Chicago: Moody Press, 1953.

Zodhiates, Spiros and Warren Baker, *The Hebrew-Greek Key Word Study Bible King James Version* (Revised Edition). Chattanooga: AMG Publishers, 1991.